BRITAIN'S ROTTENEST YEARS

BRITAIN'S ROTTENEST YEARS

DEREK WILSON

CB

First published in 2009 by

Short Books

3A Exmouth House

Pine Street

EC1R 0JH

10 9 8 7 6 5 4 3 2 1

A CIP catalogue record for this book
is available from the British Library.

ISBN 978-1-906021-58-0

Printed in Great Britain by Clays, Suffolk

Every effort has been made to obtain permission
for the material reproduced in the book. If any
errors have unwittingly occurred, we will be
happy to correct them in future editions.

CONTENTS

INTRODUCTION

Oh, don't the days seem lank and long
When all goes right and nothing goes wrong,
And isn't your life extremely flat
With nothing whatever to grumble at!

WE CURRENTLY LIVE in a pessimist's paradise such as would have warmed the heart of King Gama in Gilbert and Sullivan's *Princess Ida*. He would have found plenty to grumble at. Times is 'ard and the media delightedly lead us by our corporate nose in discovering who's to blame. It is, of course, THEM, a label to be stuck at will on greedy bankers, corrupt politicians, dishonest corporate finance bosses, or anyone else onto whom we want to shrug off our own respon-sibility for the mess we find ourselves in.

Well, that's a game I've no interest in playing. If histori-ans have any *raisons d'être* one of them should certainly be helping people to see things in perspective. Our memories tend to be short. We know that we are worse off than we were five or ten years ago and we assume that the sky is about to fall in. It ain't! We will recover. The good times will return – and will stay with us until the next recession or natural disaster or international crisis. Why can I proclaim that so confidently? Because human beings are amazingly resilient. How do I know that? Because I'm a historian. Like all historians, I take the longer view. And in this little book I want to encourage you to take the longer view. Lost your job? Seen your pension pot dry up? Business suffering from financial malnutrition? That is very hard. But your ancestors put up with things that were a hell of a lot worse. And they, or their children, survived (otherwise you wouldn't be here). As a nation we've come through some horrendous times – invasion, plague, civil war, financial collapse, rebellion, tyrannical government. But here we still are. And not only have we survived; the vast majority of us live lives that are longer, more comfortable and more varied than those of most of the generations that have passed.

In the following chapters I have highlighted some of the years in our history which were black in the extreme. To most contemporaries it seemed that their situation was irredeemable. The 'good old days' were long distant. The country was going to the dogs. Pessimists could well claim 'The future isn't what it was and the past isn't getting any better'. My aim in drawing attention to these depressing episodes in our history is not to spread yet more gloom – a dollop of black icing over a cake that seems to have lost much of its taste. I take a leaf from the writings of the nineteenth-century poet Arthur Hugh Clough. The popular view of the Victorian age is one of imperial grandeur and technical progress. It didn't strike everyone that way at the time. Clough, one of the popular poets of the day, felt the need to offer his contemporaries a pick-me-up:

> *Say not the struggle nought availeth,*
> *The labour and the wounds are vain,*
> *The enemy faints not nor faileth,*
> *And as things have been, things remain.*
> *If hopes were dupes, fears may be liars…*

In our past things have been very much worse and there's a fair to middling chance that they'll get better in the future.

What Happened Before...

AD60

When I was ten, I read fairy tales in secret, and would have been ashamed of being found doing so. Now that I am fifty, I read them openly. When I became a man, I put away childish things, including the fear of childishness and the desire to be very grown up.

WHAT WAS C.S. LEWIS getting at when he wrote the above?

He was, I think, urging upon an age intoxicated with its scientific 'grown-up-ness' the importance of myth. It was, and is, an important message. One of the notorious falsehoods of modern life is that we have outgrown religion, romance, tales of heroism and legends about the past. We have been conned by rationalists into believing that anything we can't prove or get our heads round is 'untrue' or unworthy of consideration by sophisticated adults. The reality is that we desperately need myths. When we discard the old ones, we immediately replace them with new fables about heroines and heroes of our own devising, whether fictional or real – James Bond, the inhabitants of Albert Square, or the celebrities on the cover of *Hello* magazine. Myths are not untruths. Quite the reverse; they are the stories that reveal 'us' to ourselves; that explain our ambitions and our phobias; that flesh out our identity. So there can be few things more tragic than a society stripped of its myths – or at least of those whose job it is to record and publicise them. This is what happened in Britain in AD60 when the Druids, the guardians of our ancient pagan identity, were literally wiped out.

Conquest has three phases. The first is military. The victims are humiliated in battle, lose many of their warriors and see their leaders slain in the field or executed later. Then comes indoctrination. Traditional shrines and temples are pulled down. Ancient rituals are outlawed. The conquerors erect their own temples or churches and oblige the subject peoples to worship new (and obviously superior) deities. Finally, the long process of assimilation ensues. The majority population have no choice but to accept the ways of the invaders if they wish to survive or even to prosper under the new regime. By this process empires are built. But colonisation is not usually a one-way street. Take, for example the nineteenth-century 'scramble for Africa'. Christian missionaries played a major part in the eradication of animism and ritual magic. Yet the new Christian churches that emerged there have a very distinct flavour in which traditional local music, dancing and fervour are prominent. A visitor from another planet beholding a solemn papal mass in Rome and a raucous hand-clapping service in a South African township would take some convincing that these were manifestations of the same religion. Such examples only put into perspective the enormity of what happened in Britain in AD60. The thriving local culture was so obliterated that, despite the endeavours of historians and archaeologists, we don't have much idea of what it was like.

We are under a double disadvantage in that the only reports we have of life in Celtic Britain were written by the Roman conquerors and they clearly did not understand the Celts at all. When the armies and administrators of the great Mediterranean empire ventured north over the Alps, they encountered a variety of tribes whose languages and customs were quite alien to them. They lumped them all together as 'barbarians', literally people whose languages were uncouth. These wild tribesmen were technologically backward and, in the view of the Romans, in need of becoming civilised. Even the more fair-minded chroniclers looked down on the northern 'savages' and were prone to putting the worst interpretation on what they discovered among the forests, mountains and marshes of the north. For example, some claimed that the Celts (the tribes who lived on the mainland and islands west of the Rhine) practised human sacrifice. Diodorus Siculus, writing in the first century BC, stated that 'in very important matters they prepare a human victim, plunging a dagger into his chest; by observing the way his limbs convulse as he falls and the gushing of his blood, they are able to read the future'. But Diodorus was only repeating stories he had been told and there is no unequivocal archaeological evidence to support this claim. Other rumours circulating in the Roman world told of the 'wicker man', a cage in which offenders were burned during major festivals. Again, we only have the Romans' word for it. Quite why they should have categorised such customs, if they existed, as 'barbaric' when they made public entertainments out of throwing criminals to the lions or inflicting lingering executions by crucifixion, is a mystery.

Julius Caesar gave the most detailed, first-hand account of Celtic civilisation based on his campaigns in Gaul (roughly modern France and western Germany) in 58-50BC. Caesar was most interested in the military aspects of the peoples and terrain of Europe. He wanted to understand what it was that made the Celts such ferocious warriors. This is what he concluded:

> … the main object of all education is, in their opinion, to imbue the scholars with a firm belief in the indestructibility of the human soul, which, according to their belief, merely passes at death from one tenement to another; for by such doctrine alone, they say, which robs death of all its terrors, can the highest form of human courage be developed.

We in the 21st century who read of the atrocities committed by suicide bombers can easily recognise this feature of religious nationalism: radical teachers who imbue young fundamentalist Muslims with a love of martyrdom and convince them that it is the gateway to the delights of paradise.

There was a basic culture clash between Romans and Celts and it went so deep that the conquerors were faced with a very clear choice as they advanced through Gaul to cross the narrow straits that separated Gaul from what they called Britannia: they could either bypass the Celtic territory or wipe the cultural slate clean in order to impose the Roman way of life. In other outposts of empire, the new rulers were quite prepared to live with the customs of the indigenous peoples. Indeed, they tended to respect their religious rites and beliefs; the last thing they wanted to do was anger the tribal gods. So what was so different about the Celts? The answer is Druidism. The emperors Augustus, Tiberius and Claudius all hated the religion, and delivered edicts against it.

Who, then, were the Druids, and what threat did they pose to the imperial power? Forget bearded figures in white robes and sandals wailing and chanting to welcome the sunrise over stone circles. These are fanciful rituals dreamed up by eighteenth and nineteenth-century romantics. Certainly, no Roman legionary would have quaked in his boots when confronted by such a sight. Nor would emperors have deemed it necessary to ban them and their practices on pain of death. No, the original Druids were at once more inspiring and much more terrifying.

In some ways, it is easier to say what the Druids were *not*, rather than what they were. The nearest modern point of reference is probably fundamentalist Islam and its teachers and preachers. In extremist mosques, charismatic orators rant hatred of the West and in radical *madrassas* (Qur'an schools) firebrand mullahs inspire impressionable young students to wage jihad against infidels. The instruction they give is based (some would say inaccurately) on the teaching of Muhammad and the collected wisdom of centuries of scholarship as preserved in sacred writings. Such precepts have the force of law and provide the guidelines for shari'a, literally 'the way' or 'the right path'. The corpus of the teaching embraces antiquarian study, theology and law and has political overtones. In a sense it may be said to represent the 'soul' of Islam, or, at least, of one strand of Islam. Druidism seems to have been all this and more for the Celtic peoples.

Individualism has become so central to Western society and any sense of community so watered down that it is difficult for us to get our heads round the idea that the preservation of common values, standards and beliefs can be entrusted to specialists who exist for that purpose alone. Whether or not this indicates that we are more 'advanced' and 'sophisticated' than our ancestors is very much open to debate. What is beyond doubt is that, historically, we are in the minority. Throughout the long millennia behind us magi, soothsayers, priests, shamans and holy men have been integral to the cohesion of virtually all societies.

The Druids were a priestly caste and the first thing that made the Romans wary of them was that they were drawn from across all of the Celtic tribes and were thus a unifying factor throughout the region. They were held in great awe by their people. For example, if two rival tribes were locked in battle the appearance of a druid in their midst would result in an immediate end to hostilities. This was because they were believed to be intermediaries between the people and the gods. It is a feature of most religions, including the more primitive forms of Christianity, to allot real power to priests and holy men (and women). The people are willing to give up some of the authority over their own lives because they believe they benefit from the incantations and mystic powers of their priests or elders. In a period when there was little distinction between knowledge and magic, the Druids were respected for their possession of dark secrets about both the earthly and the spiritual world. Their privileged position in society did not come unearned. Trainees were recruited early and spent many years learning ancient law by rote and being initiated into the mysteries of their religion. In a preliterary age it was the Druids who preserved all the stories of past heroes and kings and repeated them in songs and tales recited at communal feasts. It was they who kept in their heads the body of law passed down from age to age. It was they who heard appeals for justice and pronounced judgement on offenders. Once a Druid had given his verdict there was no appeal against it. We don't know whether capital punishment lay within their remit but excommunication certainly did and that was as good as a sentence of death, for then a man was cast adrift from his community he entered limbo and became a non-person. Thus the Druids were priests, scholars, poets, lawyers, judges, recorders of the past and foretellers of the future all rolled into one.

Druidical activity was centred at 'holy' sites – groves, caves and lakes – throughout western Europe but the priests were peripatetic, constantly communing with their colleagues in other tribes. They may well have had a 'headquarters' near Chartres, where an annual 'convention' was held. In Britain the main Druidical powerhouse was on the island of Anglesey, known two thousand years ago as Ynys Môn. This sacred isle, perched on the farthest coast of Britain, assumed an enhanced importance as Rome's imperial boundary edged westwards, bringing the continental tribes under closer control. It was the last stronghold of Druidism.

Julius Caesar famously 'came, saw and conquered' Britain in 55-54BC. He established Roman overlordship in the southern part of the country, then left to deal with problems in the Mediterranean, becoming sole ruler of Rome, and eventually getting himself assassinated. For many, many years, the British were left largely to their own devices with local chieftains acting as deputies for the distant imperial authority. Like the Romans, they were engrossed in their own wars and rivalries. Live and let live was the prevailing policy in Rome. Occasionally an emperor would decide that the British should be brought under tighter control but, not for the last time, the 22 miles of sea between Calais and Dover saved the islanders. The prospect of ferrying across the narrows an army which, once landed, would find retreat difficult was daunting. It wasn't until the reign of Claudius (AD42-54) that a ruler appeared who was determined to add the full conquest of 'barbarians beyond the ocean' to his CV. But the work of subjection, begun in 43, proceeded slowly. The invaders worked on the 'divide and rule' principle, drawing some tribes into alliance, while overpowering others, and exploiting existing inter-tribal rivalries wherever possible.

The Druids knew that, without cohesion, the British had little hope of repelling the superior military might of the Roman legions. So they focused all their efforts on trying to keep people together. They supported the Catuvellauni chief, Caratacus, who after he was defeated in 43 in what is now the Midlands, withdrew to Wales, from where he waged guerrilla warfare against the Romans until his final capture in 50. From Ynys Môr came promises of supernatural aid and more tangible assistance in the shape of training for freedom fighters. It's fascinating to think that over the next couple of decades Rome was forced to deal, simultaneously, with two minority religions. At the eastern end of the empire a tiny Jewish sect was founded which, within a very few years, was making a nuisance of itself in several places around the Mediterranean. In the extreme west, an ancient cult was proving decidedly obnoxious. Emperors castigated followers of both religions as enemies of the state, people whose beliefs and actions threatened to undermine what Rome stood for. They determined to exterminate them both. With Druidism they eventually succeeded. With Christianity they failed.

Still, during the AD40s, subduing Britannia proved to be an uphill task. The tribal chiefs were as slippery as soap, always calculating what was in their best interests. They lived at peace with their Roman overlords as long as the rewards for compliance were attractive. If the foreigners kept them on their thrones by supporting them against their external and internal enemies, they saw no reason to rebel. But as soon as the Roman forces in a certain area showed signs of weakness or there appeared a real prospect of forging a strong enough alliance to repel them, they would turn suddenly against their protectors. The Romans in their fortified encampments and walled settlements could never feel secure. Governors constantly had to calculate whether to employ the carrot or the stick. Legions were kept busy in various parts of the country responding to signs of unrest – not always successfully. The Silures, a tribe who occupied what is now south Wales and the border, were particularly troublesome and it is no coincidence that their country was not far from Ynys Môr.

The situation was so finely balanced that, after the Emperor Claudius was poisoned in 54, the Roman senate was divided about the wisdom of continuing the occupation of this troublesome offshore island. But Nero, who succeeded his stepfather, decided that to abandon Britannia would be humiliating. A new strategy was formed. Now there was to be no shilly-shallying with the organisers and preachers of

British terrorism. The Druids would be dealt with. The new governor, Quintus Veranius, was despatched with instructions to make this his priority. Veranius was chosen because of his successful campaigning in mountainous terrain in the Near East, experience which would be useful as he led his men through north Wales. Unfortunately, he died after only a year in office.

His replacement was another soldier with a distinguished career in mountain warfare in north Africa. Suetonius Paulinus was something of a celebrity, having been the first Roman commander to cross the Atlas Mountains. He arrived in Britain in 58, a ruthless career soldier bent on enhancing his already considerable reputation. According to the historian Tacitus, Paulinus was driven by an intense rivalry with another general, Gnaeus Domitius Corbulo, whose outstanding achievements included restoring Roman rule in Armenia. Whatever his skills as a soldier, Paulinus lacked the political dexterity required of a provincial governor and while he was fighting his way single-mindedly across the Welsh mountains to Anglesey, he pretty much left his underlings in other parts of the country to deal with the British as they saw fit. It was their insensitivity that provoked the crisis of AD60.

Much of East Anglia at that time comprised the tribal lands of the Iceni, ruled by the client chief, Prasutagus. He was one of the rulers who had done a deal with the Romans. In return for acknowledging Caesar as his overlord and paying his taxes, he was allowed to exercise rule over his people. It was the kind of relationship open to variable interpretations and the Romans and the Iceni chose to understand the rules differently. Just how differently emerged when

Prasutagus died in 60. He left a will dividing his territory between the Emperor Nero and his two daughters. According to the provincial procurator, Catus Decianus, Prasutagus had no right to make any such provision. All his land belonged to the Emperor. Roman soldiers and officials had long looked upon the possessions of this wealthy barbarian with envy and only needed a pretext to plunder at will. The late chief's presumption gave them the green light, especially as the Iceni now had no man to lead them. What resistance could Prasutagus' widow and daughters possibly put up? Tacitus recorded with distaste the behaviour of his fellow Romans:

> ... his kingdom was plundered by centurions, his house by slaves, as if they were the spoils of war. First his wife, Boudicca, was whipped and his daughters defiled. All the chief men of the Iceni, as if Rome had received the whole country as a gift, were stripped of their ancestral possessions and the king's relatives were made slaves.

This was not only a moral outrage and a violation of Rome's own laws; it was politically inept. Decianus had chosen to provoke a confrontation at the very time that the governor and all his best troops were far away. Boudicca, a highly intelligent woman and less well disposed towards the Romans than her late husband had been, was well aware of the strategic advantage her people had. The Iceni and their neighbours had long suffered from the arrogance of the occupying power. They were more than ready to answer the Queen's call to arms. So were the neighbouring Trinovantes, who had their own reasons for discontent. The invaders had established a colony for retired soldiers at Camulodunum (Colchester). The veterans had then taken over Trinovantes lands for their own farms and estates. The original owners of the land found themselves working that same land for their new masters. To add insult to injury, many of the local people had been set to work building a temple to the deified Claudius. The Trinovantes could see this only as a permanent symbol of their subjection. More recent history provides us with well documented parallels of just how resentful the British must have felt. To take one example, land confiscation in the Kenyan 'White Highlands' led to the Mau-Mau rebellion of the 1950s, with all its attendant atrocities on both sides.

The wronged Queen Boudicca took upon herself the leadership of a confederation of tribes and launched the most serious uprising the Romans ever had to face in half a millennium of occupation. The major events were narrated in detail by the historian, Cassius Dio, in the next century. He described the Queen as 'very tall, in appearance most terrifying, in the glance of her eye most fierce, and her voice was harsh; a great mass of the tawniest hair fell to her hips; around her neck was a large golden necklace; and she wore a tunic of various colours over which a thick mantle was fastened with a brooch'. It was Dio who put into Boudicca's mouth a long speech, supposedly delivered to the heads of the participating tribes, which reads like a stirring nationalist manifesto. Having listed the Romans' crimes, she then appealed to her hearers as sharers in a common destiny:

> …although we inhabit so large an island, or rather a continent, one might say, that is encircled by the sea, and although we possess a veritable world of our own and are so separated by the ocean from all the rest of mankind that we have been believed to dwell on a different earth and under

THE TRIBES OF
ANCIENT BRITAIN

CORNOVI
CAERENI
SMERTAE LUGI
DECANTAE
TAEZALI
VACOMAGI
CALEDONII
VENICONES
DAMNONI
OTAOINI
EPIDII
SELGOVAE
NOVANTAE

BRIGANTES
EBURACUM
(YORK)
PARISI
YNYS MOR
(ANGLESEA)
LINDUM (LINCOLN)
DECEANGLI • DEVA (CHESTER)
CORNOVII
CORITANI
ORDOVICES
ICENI
CATUVELLAUNI
DOBUNNI
TRINOVANTES
DEMETAE
SILURES
• GLEVUM
(GLOUCESTER)
CAMULODUNUM
(COLCHESTER)
CAERLEON
• VERULAMIUM (ST ALBANS)
TRABATES
LONDINIUM •
(LONDON)
BELGAE
REGNENSESS
CANTI
DUROTRIGES
DUMNONII

a different sky, and that some of the outside world, aye, even their wisest men, have not hitherto known for a certainty even by what name we are called, we have, notwithstanding all this, been despised and trampled underfoot by men who know nothing else than how to secure gain. However, even at this late day, though we have not done so before, let us, my countrymen and friends and kinsmen – for I consider you all kinsmen, seeing that you inhabit a single island and are called by one common name – let us, I say, do our duty while we still remember what freedom is, that we may leave to our children not only its appellation but also its reality. For, if we utterly forget the happy state in which we were born and bred, what, pray, will they do who are reared in bondage?

Stirring stuff, even though it reflects a later view of the political realities of first-century Britain. It is on the descriptions of Dio and Tacitus that the popular, multi-hued cult of Boudicca has been based – the personification of Britannia, the feminist heroine, the feisty charioteer whose statue dominates the northern end of Westminster Bridge. She must, indeed, have been a remarkable woman, but the very few facts we have about her allow us to say little more than that she became the conduit for an electrical charge of anger and resentment which had been stored up for years in occupied Britain.

This was not a war; it was a culture clash, a struggle to the death between two irreconcilable ways of life.

Rome's power base was south-east England, where the conquerors enjoyed the support of the local population. The 'hawks' believed that their urban centres, such as Londinium (London) and Camulodunum, were secure and that from them the spread of 'civilisation' was only a matter of time and superior military might. They were about to get a nasty shock.

Boudicca's horde set out for Camulodunum in a frenzy of vengeance. The Roman residents sent urgent messages to Paulinus. He ordered Petillius Cerealis, commander of the Ninth Legion, to suppress the revolt, and Cerealis duly marched his men from the West Country. His force − 2,000 infantry and 500 cavalry − was comparatively small but it should, at least, have stopped Boudicca's people in their tracks until reinforcements could arrive. It never reached the threatened colony. Somewhere in the wooded wilds of Essex it was ambushed. The British warriors cut the Ninth to pieces. Cerealis was lucky to escape with some of his cavalry. The procurator in London, Decianus, decided that this was the moment to abandon his post and he fled to Gaul. The only succour the people of Camulodunum received was 200 troops sent from Londinium by Decianus before his hasty departure. It was woefully inadequate, as were the town's defences. Camulodunum was not protected by a strong stockade − evidence, perhaps, of the townsmen's over-confidence and their contempt for the military capabilities of the British. So astonished were the colonists at the news of the rising that their traditional tactical ability seems to have deserted them. They made no clear plans for their own defence. They did not even send their women and children away to safety. Their panic was encouraged by local people within the town who spread morale-busting rumours.

Boudicca and her people made short work of the ramparts. They surged through the tidily laid-out streets and market places of the colony. The only building in which the inhabitants could find refuge was the still-unfinished Temple of Claudius, and here survivors crowded in – retired soldiers, their wives, their children and their slaves. Boudicca's warriors surrounded it. They sent continuous volleys of spears over the walls and set fire to brushwood piled outside, fanning clouds of choking smoke into the temple courtyard. Two days later, they managed to break in. What followed was an orgy of violence that demonstrated to the Romans 'anything you can do we can do better'. All the usual accompaniments of siege warfare were visited on Camulodunum – murder, rape, fire, pillage – but one outrage in particular was singled out for comment by the historians:

> The worst and most bestial atrocity committed by the captors was the following. They hung up naked the noblest and most distinguished women and then cut off their breasts andsewed them to their mouths, in order to make the victims appear to be eating them; afterwards they impaled the women on sharp skewers run lengthwise through the entire body.

It is tempting to believe that the Roman women were singled out for such treatment as a reprisal for the indignities to which Boudicca and her daughters had been subjected but it seems unlikely that the Queen would have been able to direct and control the behaviour of her followers, drunk with victory. Now they were ready for the even more vulnerable Londinium.

In the meantime, however, Paulinus had finished his work in Wales – a rampage which matched for bloodiness whatever Boudicca's horde had perpetrated. Having subdued the tribes of the borders and central Wales, he spent the winter of 59-60 at Deva (Chester) training and equipping his troops

CASSIUS DIO DESCRIBED BOUDICCA AS 'VERY TALL, IN
APPEARANCE MOST TERRIFYING, IN THE GLANCE OF HER
EYE MOST FIERCE, AND HER VOICE WAS HARSH'

for the final push into Snowdonia and Anglesey. Archaeological discoveries hint that the Druids were also preparing in their own way for a showdown. In the 1940s, an area of bog on Anglesey was excavated for wartime construction purposes. During the process, 150 first-century metal objects were recovered, most of them connected with warfare. There were chariots and horse harnesses, swords, spears and a chain used for manacling together groups of slaves or prisoners. There is no doubt that very many more artefacts would have been located if a full archaeological survey had been possible. It was not just the number of items that was remarkable; they came from several tribes and from virtually the whole of Britannia. What did this cache mean? In the first century the bog was a lake. The precious items had probably been cast into it as offerings to the gods. The rituals would have been presided over by the Druids and the military nature of the finds suggests that they were carried out in connection with war. Were the Druids summoning supernatural hosts to combat the Romans? Were they coordinating a countrywide insurrection? We may never know. What is clear is that Paulinus was right to regard Ynys Môr as absolutely crucial in the subjugation of the British tribes.

As soon as winter had lost its grip on the mountains ,,Paulinus made for the Menai Straits. He had built flat-bottomed boats to convey his infantry across to the island. The men and horses of the cavalry had to swim. The Druids and their supporters were waiting for them.

> On the beach stood the enemy forces with their dense ranks of armed warriors, while between the ranks darted women, dressed in black like the Furies with dishevelled hair and brandishing torches. At the same time the Druids, raising their hands to the heavens and spewing dreadful imprecations, terrified our soldiers with the awesome sight so that they were paralysed with fear, standing motionless and exposing themselves to wounds.

Paulinus had to pep-talk the men out of their superstitious torpor. He reminded them that they were battle-hardened Roman soldiers, not raw recruits easily cowed by shrieking women. At that the legionaries surged forward in disciplined ranks. It was the turning point – not just of the battle or even of the campaign but of the history of Roman Britain. It was the moment when the two cultures finally came face to face. If the Romans had buckled, the military and propaganda consequences would have been momentous. But once Paulinus had steeled his troops for battle, the outcome was not in doubt. The legionaries hacked down their opponents mercilessly, then set fire to the sacred groves. This was the death blow to Druidism.

The religion did not disappear immediately. For a while, in various parts of the country, practitioners carried out the ancient mysteries in secret. But lack of continuity put an end to the old priestcraft. Without teaching centres where Celtic lore could be passed on to a new generation, the unwritten secrets of the Druids soon slipped into oblivion.

Similarly, the last military expression of British independence was about to be silenced. Paulinus hurried eastwards to confront Boudicca and the rebels. He travelled ahead of the army with a personal escort to assess the situation for himself. He was met by envoys from the terrified citizenry of Londinium. They knew that they were next on the rebels' target list and they begged him to protect them. Paulinus reviewed the strategic situation dispassionately. Londinium, he concluded, was indefensible. Moreover, he could not face the enemy until he had gathered a much larger force. He decided to withdraw. All he could offer the men and women of Londinium was the opportunity to leave with his troops. As Tacitus recalled, 'Those who were chained to the spot by the weakness of their sex or the infirmity of age or the attractions of the place were cut off by the enemy.' For the first time Britain's future capital was sacked.

It was, in fact, the lack of discipline among the British tribesmen that proved their undoing. While Paulinus thought ahead and made tough decisions, Boudicca's people gave themselves up to plunder. They fell crazedly on soft targets where they unleashed their fury against civilians and carried off wagonloads of booty. They bypassed Roman garrisons which they might easily have overrun, thus denying refuge to Paulinus' men and establishing bases for themselves. They fragmented into small bands to attack small settlements and homesteads. Drunk (sometimes literally) with their success, they made every Roman they could find pay for the indignities and hardships they had so long endured. Boudicca simply could not hold her large host together. Their next main target was Verulamium (St Albans) which soon shared the fate of Camulodunum and Londinium. Again, Paulinus lifted no finger to aid the stricken settlement. He was deliberately playing the long game. Tacitus estimated Roman losses at 70,000. He pointed out that the British were uninterested in the normal customs of war, such as taking prisoners and holding them to ransom: 'They wasted no time in getting down to the bloody business of hanging, burning and crucifying. It was as if they feared that retribution might catch up with them while their vengeance was only half complete.' The historian's assessment was, surely, correct. This was not war; it was a culture clash, a struggle to the death between two irreconcilable ways of life.

The exultant British horde marched westwards, leaving a trail of burning buildings and unburied bodies. They were now eager for their meeting with Caesar's representative and the meagre body of troops under his command. Certain of victory. Confident of regaining their independence.

Paulinus certainly did not take for granted the outcome of his forthcoming confrontation with Boudicca. The governor realised that that confrontation must take place sooner rather than later. To wait several weeks for reinforcements from Gaul would be to leave the initiative with the enemy, by which time Boudicca's host would undoubtedly have been joined by other tribes eager to grab their own freedom. Paulinus sent messengers to every available commander to bring their men to his standard. He was only able to assemble an army of about 10,000-12,000 from the Fourteenth and Twentieth Legions and auxiliaries from nearby garrisons, and needed every extra man he could muster. The fragility of his position was brought home to him when Poenius Postumus, commanding the Second Legion, stationed at Exeter, refused his summons. Postumus was the camp prefect, that is to say, he was third in rank. He was well aware of the precarious situation in the south west and may well have considered it unwise to remove the entire Exeter garrison. His evaluation of the overall situation was, presumably, that the governor was doomed and that, rather than joining him in a 'death or glory' fight with the massive forces coming against him from East Anglia, he should keep his legion intact for future action.

Paulinus had to make the best of a bad job, relying on intelligent tactics and the bravery of his soldiers. He could, at least, choose the site for the battle. He decided to make his stand near modern Lichfield. He found an excellent defensive position, a narrow defile with woods to the rear and along both sides commanding an open plain to the east. In such a situation the enemy's numbers might not actually be to their disadvantage. As they approached, their front would get narrower and provide an easier target for Roman javelins. The contest would then be between a small force of calm, well-disciplined troops and a mighty, excited rabble. Dio says that the British horde numbered 230,000. That is an impossibly high estimate but undoubtedly the Romans were massively outnumbered.

Well trained and battle-hardened though Paulinus' troops were, they must have been nervous at the first sight of their approaching foe. Boudicca's force spread out over the plain, a fast incoming tide of spear-waving, defiance-screaming warriors, chariots to the fore. Behind them came their families and their wagons, piled high with booty. The women and children now took up vantage points to watch the crushing defeat of their oppressors.

The governor rode out before his men to steel them for the fray. Roman historians could never allow their accounts of battles to begin without the making of stirring speeches. According to Tacitus, Paulinus addressed his small 'band of brothers' in words reminiscent of those later put by Shakespeare into the mouth of Henry V before Agincourt:

> Ignore the noises and empty threats made by these savages. There are more women than men in their ranks. They have no armour or proper weapons and will break when they feel your steel and sense the courage of men who have beaten them so many times already. What glory lies before you, an elect few who will gather the laurels of a whole army!
> ...Keep close order. When you have thrown your javelins, push forward with the bosses of your shields and swords. Let the dead pile up. Forget all about plunder. Win the victory and everything will be yours.

The British host came to a halt. If there was any tactical point to their brayed taunts and brandishing of weapons it was to draw the Romans out from their position into the open. But Paulinus' men held their ground. It was a stand-off. Whose resolve would break first? The answer would be decided by the quality of leadership in the two armies and the reality was that the British lacked leadership. They were a loose confederation of tribes, each with its own chief. There is no indication in the records that Boudicca had any tactical skill or that she made any attempt to direct the course of the battle. She was an inspiring figurehead and Tacitus credits her with a long speech but she was unable to control her huge, disparate army. In fact, the task would have tested the most experienced of generals. The rolling tide of over-confident warriors could not be held back. It was only a matter of time before they broke ranks and rushed forward, eager to get at the enemy. With their trumpets blaring and their chiefs calling out to the gods for aid, Boudicca's chariots surged across the open ground, followed by the infantry in a running charge.

At the American Civil War battle of Bunker Hill, General Israel Putnam is reputed to have ordered his Confederate troops not to fire until they could see the whites of their enemies' eyes. Paulinus must have issued a similar instruction, for none of his men made a move as the intimidating multitude of tribesmen surged towards them. Then, when they were a mere 40 paces away, he ordered them to loose their javelins. Some 7,000 steel shafts flew into the air and rained down on the advancing British. A second volley immediately followed. Instant confusion. Dead and wounded men and horses littered the ground. Those coming behind could not avoid stumbling over the bodies. Paulinus gave them no opportunity to retreat or regroup. He called to his men to charge. In wedge formation, protected by their long shields, the Romans moved smoothly forward like a human tank, ploughing into the panicking British and laying about them with their short swords. Then came the cavalry. Riding out to right and left, they encircled the heaving mass. Everywhere Boudicca's men looked they saw helmeted Romans and felt the sharp edge of their weapons. Those able to turn and run now found their retreat cut off by their own wagons and terrified families. Yet the battle did not end in a speedy rout. The British warriors were not lacking in courage and, even after their initial reverse, they still had numerical superiority. So, the conflict became a bloody, clanging mêlée of hand-to-hand encounters. Only as the day drew to a close and stragglers were able to take advantage of the failing light to escape could Paulinus end the action and survey the corpse-strewn ground.

What he saw, according to the official account, was 80,000 British dead and 400 Romans. The figures lack credibility. History is always written by the victors, and Paulinus had every reason to massage the figures in his report to Rome. The battle had been, as Wellington said of Waterloo, 'a damn close thing'. So it should have been. This was the final reckoning between two mighty civilisations. The Celts lost and would before long be driven into the fringes of mainland Britain. Rome tightened its grip on all the tribal areas south of the walls that later emperors would eventually build as boundaries against the Caledonian tribes. With varying degrees of reluctance or enthusiasm, the conquered people would learn a new language, new ways, new laws, new values. After AD60 nothing would ever be the same again — although, ironically, *both* the Romans and their British subjects would eventually be conquered by that alien movement that was emerging at the other end of the empire — Christianity. The nineteenth-century poet, Algernon Swinburne, lamented the passing of the pagan world and the triumph of Christianity:

> *Though the feet of thine high priests tread where thy lords and our forefathers trod,*
> *Though these that were gods are dead and thou, being dead, art a god...*
> *Yet thy kingdom shall pass, Galilean, thy dead shall go down to thee dead.*

Swinburne was just one of the many writers who idealised the pagan past. For them, Boudicca became a national hero-ine and the Druids guardians of a store of ancient wisdom, now regrettably lost. What was the reality — such as we can reconstruct? The Queen of the Iceni's star blazed very briefly in the twilight of Celtic civilisation. Her end, appar-ently, came shortly after the final battle, either as a result of poison or a broken heart. The Druids never recovered their power after the destruction of their groves on Ynys Môr. I don't believe either was a great loss. They were people of a violent age who, no less than the Romans who displaced them, dealt in death and spoke the language of vengeance. And our sympathy and admiration for men and women who go down fighting for a cause they believe in does not oblige us to approve of that cause. But it's not my task to moralise. What is clear is that AD60 witnessed a traumatic end to the ancient British way of life.

What Happened Before...

1069   ROTTENEST YEAR

1069

IMMIGRATION – ILLEGAL OR OTHERWISE – has always been a feature of life in Britain. Those few miles of English Channel seem to have presented a challenge to people looking for a better life than they had in continental Europe. After the Romans, wave after wave of settlers came across throughout the next millennium. Almost exactly 1,000 years after Paulinus' arrival, another man of war brought an army to our shores. His name was Guillaume le Bâtard. We call him William the Conqueror. And, as every schoolboy knows, or used to know, he defeated the reigning English King, Harold, at the Battle of Hastings in 1066 and marked his victory by commissioning the first strip cartoon in history – the Bayeux Tapestry (actually, it was his half-brother, Odo, who ordered it).

One invasion; one battle; and England stopped being Anglo-Saxon and became part of the Norman empire.Right? Wrong. Life is never that simple. Conquest isn't a matter of a few hundred horsemen and archers knocking the stuffing out of their opponents. It takes time. It provokes resistance. It is usually very messy and very, very bloody. Anglo-Saxon resistance to William the Conqueror and his ruling elite has certainly become the stuff of legend. Victorian novelists and twentieth century Hollywood producers used it as a rich quarry for swashbuckling adventures. But, stripped of its romantic overtones, the story of 1069-70 reveals the ordeal of a people crushed beneath the heel of an occupying power. From Hadrian's Wall to the Lizard, from Anglesey to the Wash, every local community felt the force of their new political masters as they ruthlessly expunged old ruling families, old loyalties, old customs. They hit back with courage and determination.

But that is only the half of it. If the story of these months was simply the record of the brave but doomed resistance of a proud people that would be bad enough. The reality was more complex and more tragic. In the chaos of war and rebellion Englishmen fought Normans, Normans fought Irishmen, Danes fought Normans, Normans fought Scots, Englishmen fought Welshmen, Englishmen fought Englishmen, and the land took more than a generation to recover from the devastation.

The troubles began with fire and ended with fire. In January 1069 rebels in Northumbria forced their way into the city of Durham looking for the Norman governor, Robert de Commines. They tracked him down to the bishop's house where he had taken refuge and set it ablaze. Robert and several of his men were burned to death or hacked down as they tried to escape the flames. This violent act was just one of a series of desperate outrages perpetrated by men trying to rid the country of its hated Norman overlords. But were they freedom fighters or terrorists? Campaigners for a way of life that was doomed to extinction or greedy princelings trying to cling to power?

These were certainly troubled and confused times. We should not think of Europe as neatly divided into nation states with well-defined borders. Large parts of it were controlled by powerful warlords constantly competing with each other. The military impetus in the north-west came from Scandinavia, from which Viking marauders sailed to take advantage of England's long coastline and the lands on the other side of the Channel to make lightning raids or set up pirate kingdoms. These incursions and invasions had been going on for two and a half centuries. Dublin was founded in 841 as a Viking base from which raids could be launched on Celtic and Anglo-Saxon settlements on both sides of the Irish Sea. By 886 much of northern and eastern England – the Danelaw – was under the control of Scandinavian settlers. Similarly, a band of these 'Northmen' had forced the French King to acknowledge their title to what came to be called Normandy (i.e. the land of the Northmen, or Normans), which they used as a base for further raids – some as far as the Mediterranean.

Warfare between the 'thug nobility' of Britain and the nearby mainland was a constant but it was not simply a question of peaceful Anglo-Saxon farmers resisting the ravages of horn-helmeted barbarians. (Actually, the Vikings did not wear horned helmets.) Anglo-Saxon and Scandinavian rulers frequently fought among themselves and it was not unusual for a king of Wessex, for example, to hire Danish soldiers to help him ward off challenges from his own rebel subjects. All the kings and petty princelings of Europe were gang leaders who kept bands of armed retainers and held power by pitting themselves against one another. For example, it was only a few years before the Norman Conquest that Macbeth had murdered his way to the Scottish throne. Politically, at least, these were dark ages.

Somehow, amidst this turbulence, ordinary people managed to farm their holdings, sell their produce at market and maintain relations with their neighbours. It would be wrong to think of every family in the land living in daily fear of having their fields trampled and their houses burned round their ears. Communities living at a distance from the coast were relatively secure against Viking marauders and even political change at the top as a result of dynastic rivalries made little impact at the humbler social strata. English men and women lived under established laws, enforced through a hierarchy of courts. The leaders of society had a say in the selection of their kings and in the formation of policy. For most people, day-to-day living was not too bad – until their King Harold fell out with Duke William of Normandy.

The family feuding which eventually led to the Norman conquest started half a century earlier. In 1016 the English King, Ethelred II, died and left the crown to his son Edward (nicknamed the 'Confessor'). But he was shouldered aside by the Danish King, Cnut, who, already in control of the Danelaw in the north, now added Ethelred's English territory to his own. Edward took refuge with his maternal grandfather, Richard II, Duke of Normandy. In his haven beyond the Channel the dispossessed King became thoroughly 'Normanised'; and when he was eventually able to return to his own land in 1042, he came almost as a foreigner surrounded by Norman favourites. As a monarch,

Edward was totally ineffectual. He left military and political affairs largely in the hands of the Anglo-Saxon Earl Godwin and his son, Harold. The King's all-consuming passion was religion and his top priority was not defending and extending his frontiers but founding churches. Early in his reign he began the construction of new buildings for monks established just outside London at Westminster. His pursuit of personal holiness included abstaining from sexual relations with his beautiful young wife – although this may have been the result of homosexuality. It was soon obvious to all interested parties that the King would leave no heir to succeed him, and several pairs of covetous eyes began focusing on the throne. Edward had come to an arrangement with his mother's people that he would be succeeded by Duke William of Normandy; but it was always unlikely that other interested parties would sit back and allow England to be annexed to the Norman empire.

On 28 December 1065 the new abbey church at Westminster was consecrated. It was the crowning achievement of Edward's life – and the last. He was too ill to attend the ceremony and, on 5 January, he died. According to legend, with his last breath he prophesied evil days ahead for the land, as well he might. The monks of Edward's abbey ensured that his reputation for piety lived on and, less than a century later, Edward the Confessor was canonised, the only English king to be thus honoured.

With Edward out of the way, William of Normandy now prepared to enter his inheritance. However, before he could do so, Harold Godwinson, the man on the spot, beat him to it. Harold claimed that Edward had promised the crown to him. And then another contender threw his hat into the ring.

This was Harold Hardraada, King of Norway, who insisted that the previous English King, Harthacnut, had willed the throne to him.

The result of all this was that in 1066 England faced two invasions. In the late summer, aided by Harold's renegade brother, Tostig, Hardraada landed a large army on the Yorkshire coast. Harold hurried to confront it and, at the Battle of Stamford Bridge, won such a resounding and bloody victory that the Anglo-Norwegian host was decimated and both Hardraada and Tostig were killed. But Harold had no time to refresh his weary warriors. William had already landed on the Sussex coast. There he consolidated his position while Harold force-marched his army southwards.

Luck was certainly on William's side. Contrary winds had prevented his ships sailing at midsummer. Had he crossed the Channel then – i.e. before the Battle of Stamford Bridge – he would have found Harold waiting for him with his army at full strength. Equally, had the confrontation occurred later, when Harold had been able to reassemble his forces, the outcome would probably have been different. As it was, the Battle of Hastings was fought on 14 October 1066 and Harold Godwinson was killed in the field.

Everything seemed to be going William's way. He had defeated his Anglo-Saxon enemies and he was determined to rub their noses in their humiliation. He ordered a lavish coronation in Edward the Confessor's new abbey and followed this by gathering groups of leaders in several localities and forcing them to take oaths of allegiance. In March he made a triumphal procession throughout the south in which he paraded as hostages several of England's leading men.

Then he set off back to Normandy. With him he took as his 'guests' all the potential English leaders he had been able to lay hands on, including the heir presumptive, Edgar the Atheling.

William left his new realm in the hands of a few thousand Norman lords and knights who had every incentive to establish their authority by whatever means came to hand.

> The English were groaning under the Norman yoke, and suffering oppressions from the proud lords who ignored the king's injunctions. The petty lords who were guarding the castles oppressed all the native inhabitants of high and low degree, and heaped shameful burdens on them.
>
> Orderic Vitalis

But foreigners were not the only petty tyrants in England. William, a good judge of men, knew that he could rely on greed to win the support of many Anglo-Saxon lords. He made it worth their while to transfer their allegiance to him. Most land confiscated from Harold's dead warriors the victor distributed to his own countrymen, but he also made it clear that rewards were available to Englishmen who swore allegiance to the new regime.

As in any occupation situation, there were collaborators, men prepared to swallow national pride and give their support to the new gang leader. William had an almost inexhaustible bran tub of goodies to hand out. There have been two great land grabs in English history, those carried out by William I and Henry VIII. Just as Henry won support for his confiscation of Church property by distributing much of the proceeds among the ruling class, so William offered bribes to his one-time enemies. Both acts were revolutionary and both

WILDMEN

'Many men lived in tents, disdaining to sleep in houses lest they should become soft... the Normans called them "wildmen" (Latin *silvatici*).' – Orderic Vitalis (eleventh-century chronicler)'

In the eleventh-century large tracts of England and Wales were still forested and it was natural that many dispossessed Anglo-Saxons would seek refuge among the trees and dense undergrowth. These outlaw bands, living in makeshift bowers and probably clad in green-brown camouflage, were lawless thugs who had a fearsome reputation. Though they presented themselves as freedom fighters who carried out guerrilla raids on Norman castles and travellers, they were not above preying on their own people. Unsurprisingly, they gave rise to numerous legends. The 'woodwose' or 'green man' can still be seen carved in the wood or stone of medieval churches. The legend of Robin Hood probably owes its origin to an eleventh or twelfth-century hero/villain. And the story of Gawain and the Green Knight, which forms part of the Arthurian legend, may have been inspired by the *silvatici*.

carved deep divisions in English society.

What William imposed on England was martial law – permanent martial law. It is known as feudalism and it survived for most of the next 400 years. All previous landlord-tenant arrangements were swept away. Henceforth, property was used as the glue to hold together a military regime. William granted land to tenants-in-chief in return for providing specified numbers of armed men to fight his wars (or to suppress rebellion). They in turn sub-let to others on a similar basis. The whole system was geared to the maintenance of a warrior caste, a caste bound totally to the sovereign. Anglo-Saxon lords were eligible for land grants. For a fee they could remain in possession of their hereditary lands or purchase confiscated territory from the Crown. Any money that changed hands did not come out of the pockets of the landowners; it was simply collected from their tenants in the form of enforced taxes. It was a system born of violence that, in its turn, spawned violence.

There were Anglo-Saxon patriots who were determined not to go down without a fight. To gain some kind of feel for what life was like in the early days of Norman rule we might remind ourselves of those old black-and-white newsreels made in 1940-41, showing the merciless progress of Nazi occupation in the conquered lands of western Europe. Like the resistance fighters then, many outlaws took to the forests and became what the Normans contemptuously called *silvatici*, 'wildmen', lawless brigands who had about them a heroic and romantic air and who have lived on in legend right down to the present day in Hollywood swashbuckling epics. To us the originals of these tales are, in most cases, no more than names – Edric the Wild, who harried the Welsh borderlands; Godwin, Maagnus and Edmund, sons of Harold Godwinson, who skulked in Ireland and from there launched raids against south-west England; Skalpi, who joined the host at York and perhaps died there; another Edric, who escaped to Denmark and, best known of all, Hereward the Wake (who in June 1070 would lead an Anglo-Danish raid on the abbey and town of Peterborough and reduce it to ashes). Other opponents of the new regime adopted a more political approach. They crossed the seas in the hope of persuading foreign rulers to come to their aid. In Denmark, Sweyn Estrithson, nephew of Cnut the Great, responded to the plea and prepared an invasion fleet.

Edgar the Atheling, meanwhile, had escaped from William's entourage and taken refuge with King Malcolm of Scotland. For a while there was an upsurge of hope among the English. Towards the end of 1068 Edgar sent out messages to every part of the country calling on the leaders to gather their men and bind themselves by a solemn oath to raise the standard of revolt. He ordered that prayers be said in all churches for the success of the venture. The new governor of Northumbria, Robert de Commines, was warned about the opposition but arrogantly refused to take any precautions. He believed that the way to obtain the respect of the northerners was to demonstrate defiance and contempt. Arriving in Durham at the end of 1068, he and his 500-strong entourage set about looting the city and abusing the citizenry. He, therefore, had no-one but himself to blame for the violent reaction which followed. As already mentioned, he took up residence in the bishop's house and it was there that he met his well-deserved end. Local people set fire to the timber-framed building. Robert and most of his men per-

WHO WAS
WILLIAM THE CONQUEROR?

He was a warrior-prince toughened from a very early age
by hardship. He was born around 1028, the illegitimate
elder son of Robert I, Duke of Normandy, a baron of the
kingdom of France. When William was only seven his
father died during a pilgrimage to Jerusalem. This led to
anarchy in Normandy. Rival magnates, despite having
sworn allegiance to William, tried to grab the ducal
crown from little 'William the Bastard'. No less than four
of the child's close advisers and tutors were murdered
before 1042. Even then it took another twelve years before
William became the undisputed master of his dukedom.
Putting down rebellions and dealing with powerful rivals
turned him into a skilful, courageous and ruthless military
leader. He was not the sort of man to be trifled with, as
Harold of England discovered to his cost.

ished either in the blaze or while trying to escape the conflagration.

The triumphant rebels marched south to York, the next stronghold of any consequence, and were joined there by Edgar and his host. When the Norman garrison came out to meet the insurgents they got a heavy bruising. The English were emboldened by the knowledge that William was currently in Normandy, but they seriously underestimated his tenacity and determination. As soon as news of the revolt reached him, he took ship, arrived in his kingdom, gathered his men and force-marched them all the way to York. Edgar and his followers were taken completely by surprise. They lost several hundred men in the ensuing battle. But the Atheling and his chief men lived to fight another day. They escaped back to Scotland and began recruiting more warriors for what had become a desperate civil war.

The Danish King now decided that the time had come to take advantage of the chaos. Sweyn Estrithson despatched a mighty war fleet of 240 ships under the command of his brother, Osbjorn, and his sons, Harold and Cnut. According to the best of the Anglo-Norman chronicles, Orderic Vitalis *Historia eccesiastica*, the Danish host was augmented by mercenaries from several of the lands fringing the Baltic. Whether they were intent on invasion or were simply looking for plunder is not clear. Probably its leaders were not decided on an overall strategy but would 'play it by ear'. If the Normans in any area crumbled before them and if they could make common cause with Scandinavian or English local rulers, they would settle. Otherwise, vulnerable towns and particularly monasteries offered rich pickings. The invaders began their depredations on the Kentish coast and worked their way northwards. Either they met unexpectedly firm resistance or they regarded this series of raids as merely a prelude to the main campaign, which would begin once they had linked up with Edgar and his host. This happened in late August. The Danes anchored in the Humber estuary and, within days, the two armies had merged. They set off for York and the city now experienced its third assault in a year. The Norman defenders stood little chance. Once they ventured out of their citadel, they were confronted by a hostile citizenry as well as the invaders. They were cut to pieces – but not before they had set fire to the city. Houses, castles and even the minster were consumed in the holocaust. The brief siege of York entered English legend. The exploits of the Anglo-Danish heroes were recited and sung by minstrels for generations to come – exploits such as that of Earl Waltheof who, so the story goes, laid about him so mightily with his long-handled axe that a hundred Normans fell before him. According to the chronicles, 3,000 Normans were slaughtered in the battle for York. Edgar's defeat of a few months before had been very satisfactorily avenged.

This should have marked a turning point in the fortunes of King William. The forces against him and his Norman minority were large and growing by the day. Malcolm of Scotland now threw in his lot with Edgar by marrying the Atheling's sister. Encouraged by the recapture of York, other potential rebels grabbed their chance to take to arms. In the autumn of 1069 the odds must have seemed to be on the overthrow of the Norman regime or, at least, the establishment of an independent realm covering much of the north of the country – a second Danelaw. This did not happen because William was a forceful leader and a sound military

THE GREAT FAMILY FEUD

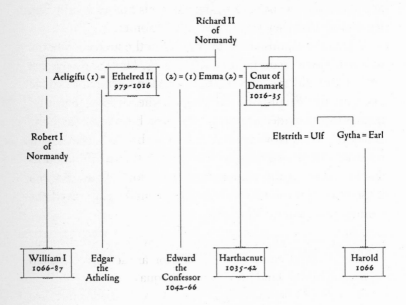

Richard II
of
Normandy

Aeligifu (1) = Ethelred II | (2) = (1) Emma (2) = Cnut of
979-1016 | | Denmark
1016-35

Robert I
of
Normandy

Elstrith = Ulf   Gytha = Earl

William I | Edgar | Edward | Harthacnut | Harold
1066-87 | the | the | 1035-42 | 1066
| Atheling | Confessor | |
| | 1042-66 | |

(The names in boxes are those who ruled as kings of England)

[52]

strategist. But it also did not happen because the leaders of the Anglo-Danish opposition could not distinguish between long-term political planning and short-term plundering. Having helped themselves to all that devastated York had to offer in the way of loot, the Danes returned to their ships and their allies went back to their various homes for the winter, feeling that they were safe for the moment.

William's response did not wait upon the arrival of better weather. Once again he hurried to York. He found it deserted but this did not prevent him wreaking a terrible vengeance on the English he did find in the stricken city and throughout a wide swathe of country beyond. The King excused the 'harrowing of the North' by the necessity of making a demonstration so memorable that its inhabitants would never again contemplate rebellion. That did not impress even those chroniclers who normally supported the Conqueror. Orderic Vitalis wrote:

> I have often felt able to commend William as his merits deserve but I cannot praise him for an act which visited famine on the land and destroyed equally the bad and the good. For I note that innocent children, young people, servants... and grey-haired elders were made destitute. I would rather sympathise with the woes and sufferings of the wretched people than attempt the unworthy task of excusing with flattering untruths the one who was guilty of such an extensive massacre... such barbaric slaughter should not go unpunished.

William I was one of the worst tyrants in history, a ruler who has a secure place in the premier league of villainy alongside Nero, Ivan the Terrible, Hitler and Stalin. He was hugely successful in everything he undertook in an age where 'success' was almost synonymous with 'ruthlessness'. He bled his subjects dry to fill his own coffers. He tore down scores of villages in the New Forest just to create a private hunting park. He knew that to survive he had to make his people fear him and he never flinched from acts of terror. But, even by his standards, the devastation of the north was an appalling – and actually unnecessary – episode. Wholesale slaughter left fields untilled and stock untended. Those who survived the purge of fire and sword faced a worse fate. Men, women and children were forced to feed on dogs, cats and rats and when they ran out the people simply died. Their unburied bodies littered the landscape. Soon, the only living creatures to be seen throughout hundreds of square miles were wild animals and brigands. It would be decades before the northern counties were repopulated. William's reputation went before him and this played a major part in deterring people from supporting the rebels. When the sons of the late King Harold attacked Bristol they were beaten off by the inhabitants. They retired to the Low Countries and disappeared from history. But other resistance fighters continued to defy their Norman overlords. Edwin the Wild, one of the *silvatici*, enlisted the aid of the Welsh King Bedwyn for an attack on Shrewsbury but, having sacked the city, they withdrew back to the safety of Snowdonia rather than face Norman reprisals.

At this time large areas of the north had yet to be subdued. William was still occupied harrying the land beyond York. West of the Pennines there were large tracts of untamed country and a hostile population far outnumbering anything the Normans could bring against them. Had the

English been able to produce a charismatic leader capable of uniting the people, the tide of invasion might have been turned. Unfortunately, Edgar the Atheling was no match for his adversary, even with the support of his father-in-law, Malcolm of Scotland. He settled with his men at Chester, intending to see out the winter of 1069-70 and face William with fresh, rested forces in the spring.

By mid-February the rebels were well settled in their winter quarters when devastating news reached the gates of Chester. Norman troops were emerging from the passes of the snow-swathed Pennines. In a remarkable demonstration of willpower and leadership, William had carried out the most audacious manoeuvre of his military career. Through fog and biting winds, through swamps and frozen rivers, the King had driven his near-mutinous men across the spinal ridge of England. When the Normans reached Chester, with its supplies of food and prospect of shelter, they were in no mood to offer quarter. The defenders were taken by surprise and put up little resistance. Fearful slaughter was visited on the city and the surrounding lands. The roads south were soon clogged with fleeing refugees. Some reached Evesham, where the monks of the abbey distributed food to the procession of starving, shivering wretches who begged their charity. Contemporary chroniclers reckoned that 100,000 people perished in the northern harrowing.

Still William's worries were not over. Back in the east, he had had to come to terms with the Danes. Unable to dislodge them from the mouth of the Humber, he had offered a bribe. In return for a substantial payment, Osbjorn agreed to sail home. He had no intention of doing anything of the sort as long as there were still rich pickings to be had in

England. By the spring the Danes had been joined by their King, Sweyn Estrithson. He moved his fleet out of the estuary and sailed southwards into the Wash. Word spread rapidly. The excited fenland people believed their saviour had come, as the *Anglo-Saxon Chronicle* records:

> The people of the countryside met him and came to terms with him, thinking that he was sure to conquer the whole country. He had with him Earl Osbjorn and Bishop Christian of Aarhus and the Danish house carls [royal guards; crack troops] and he went to Ely where Englishmen from all the fenlands came to meet them, thinking that they were sure to conquer the whole land.

This is the point at which Hereward the Wake enters the story. He was a Lincolnshire landowner, probably of Danish origin, and he now headed up the fenland resistance. Subsequent legend turned him into a great national hero who performed phenomenal feats of bravery which, in turn, were further embellished by Charles Kingsley in his popular novel of 1865 and by the Hollywood creators of filmic fiction. The few facts we possess suggest that he was a fairly typical, thuggish, axe-toting warrior. Certainly the monastic writer of the *Anglo-Saxon Chronicle* had nothing good to say about him and his companions in arms:

> Early in the morning [2 June 1070] came all the outlaws with many ships, resolved to enter [Peterborough Abbey] but the monks withstood, so that they could not come in. Then they laid on fire and burned all the houses of the monks and all the town except one house. Then they came in through fire at the Bullhithe Gate, where the monks met them and besought peace of them. But they regarded noth-

ing. They went into the minster, climbed up to the holy rood, took away the diadem from our Lord's head, all of pure gold, and seized the bracket that was underneath his feet, which was all of red gold. They climbed up the steeple, brought down the table that was hid there, which was all of gold and silver, seized two golden shrines and nine of silver and took away fifteen large crucifixes of gold and silver, and so many treasures in money, in raiment and in books as no man could tell another… Afterwards, they went to their ships, proceeded to Ely, and deposited there all the treasure…

There was more to this raid than meets the eye. It was not yet another straightforward piece of criminal rapacity. The plunderers actually claimed that they were taking away all the goodies of this rich abbey in order to protect them. 'A likely story', you might think. Both sides had their eyes on the wealth of the religious houses. The *Chronicle* tells us that 'the King ordered all the monasteries in England to be plundered'. This was the savage and rapacious act of a ruler who looked upon the people he governed, not as subjects to whom he had any obligation, but as people whose persons and property were his to do with as he pleased. The monasteries formed a prime target for a number of reasons. They contained monks, many of whom sympathised with the rebels. They were places where fugitives often sought sanctuary, believing, mistakenly, that William would not violate holy ground. They were rich in the votive offerings of generations of pious patrons. They also served as banks. If there was anywhere in the realm where wealthy Englishmen might safely deposit their movable assets, it was in the houses of prayer, where, behind stout walls, the otherworldly inmates could be trusted to guard them. The new King was about to demonstrate his contempt for man and God (at least, that is how the chroniclers, who were, of course, monks, saw things). William could argue, with some political justification, that it was necessary to confiscate the money and precious belongings of potential rebels in order to prevent them from buying arms and mercenaries. But any such special pleading was a palpably shallow excuse to cover his insatiable acquisitiveness and his fury at being resisted. He ransacked the abbeys, not only for gold and silver which could be melted down for coin, but for their ancient deeds and charters. He was determined that no-one should be able to claim rights that he had not granted. Thus humiliation and theft went hand in hand. Again, a twentieth century comparison is appropriate. Hitler's confiscation of works of art and ancient artefacts earned him the nickname 'the Jackdaw of Linz'.

The best way to ensure the passivity of the religious estab-

lishment was to ensure that its leaders were men he could trust. He arrested and imprisoned several abbots and bishops and replaced them with Normans. In the summer of 1070 he had just appointed a new abbot to Peterborough, one of his cronies by the name of Thorold, and this 'spiritual shepherd of the flock' was already on his way to assume command with a large armed retinue. Hereward had close connections with Peterborough Abbey and was certainly concerned that the Normans should not enrich themselves yet further at the monastery's expense. If we give him the benefit of the doubt, he might have been convinced that the removal of shiploads of precious religious artefacts to his headquarters at Ely was a good idea. Whatever he may have thought, however, his Danish friends were quite clear what they planned to do with the treasure. Once stowed aboard the Danish ships, it was never going to see England again.

But English hopes were not immediately dashed. Several thegns and their followers congregated at Ely, ready to defy the Conqueror, believing that from there they could mount a real national rebellion. And in this case they were in with more of a chance. Cities like York, Durham and Chester were vulnerable to fire and siege but the waterlogged fenland of East Anglia presented the Normans with a formidable problem. The Isle of Ely really was an island, its abbey-topped mound rising above a landscape of waterways and marsh. This was not the sort of country over which mounted knights could gallop and ride down their opponents. Here the masters were the local people, the 'slodgers', who alone knew the rivers and hidden causeways. William was not about to go rushing in to punish this latest act of defiance. In any case, his presence was once more needed beyond the

Channel. It was not only English subjects who found the burdens he laid on them irksome. So, in the case of Ely, he undertook to accomplish by politics what he could not achieve by force. He did a deal with King Sweyin. By its terms the Danes were allowed to sail away unmolested – and take with them the vast treasures of Peterborough and all their other plunder. Hereward and his companions were left in the lurch. The departure of the Danish host in effect marked the end of the English resistance to Norman rule.

This is where history merges into legend. The adventures of Hereward, like the later ones of Robin Hood (who entered the literature in the early fifteenth century), tell us more about the state of society in the years of Norman rule than they do about the real-life activities of flesh-and-blood heroes. The bards and ballad makers of the Middle Ages had no victorious champions to celebrate, so they celebrated magnificent failure. Hereward became the personification of defiant English pride, suppressed but never crushed by foreign tyranny. The story of the defence of Ely is full of valiant incidents, some of which must have their roots in fact. Hereward enters the enemy camp disguised as an itinerant hawker of pots to discover William's plans. He leads a nocturnal party in a raid on the King's siege towers to douse the reeds in pitch and set fire to them. When the Conqueror, by a 'divide and rule' programme of false promises and bribery eventually penetrates Ely's defences, Hereward and his loyal companions withdraw to another watery stronghold to continue the war. In fact, the determined King established his rule over this last troublesome area of his realm within months.

No more reliable is the deathbed penitence Orderic

Vitalis attributed to William. According to the pious chronicler, the dying King confessed:

> I have persecuted the native inhabitants beyond all reason...
> I have cruelly oppressed them; unjustly disinheriting many;
> multitudes... perished through me by famine or the sword.
> I fell upon the English of the northern shires like a ravening
> lion. I commanded their houses and corn and all their
> implements and chattels to be burned without distinction
> and large herds of cattle and beasts of burden to be butchered wherever they were found. It was then that I took
> revenge on multitudes of both sexes by subjecting them to
> the calamity of cruel famine. I became the barbarous murderer of many thousands, both young and old.

What is wrong with this is not the analysis of William's impact on the occupied lands but his confession of his villainy (something of a conventional set piece in ancient chronicles). Orderic used the King's supposedly troubled conscience to describe the devastation the King and his warriors visited upon the country and its people.

Equally dubious is the fourteenth-century account of confrontation between the King and the aged Archbishop Aldred of York. Aldred had officiated at the coronation of Harold and also the coronation of William. He served the latter loyally but was eventually driven to appear before the throne as the agent of divine condemnation. 'Hear me, King William,' he thundered,

> ...When you were a stranger and when God in his wrath
> against the sins of our nation granted to you to win with
> much blood the kingdom of all Britain, I consecrated you as
> king, I gave you my blessing and set the crown upon your

head. Now, because your deeds call for it, I give you my curse instead of my blessing, as to a persecutor of the Church of God, an oppressor of her ministers, as one who has broken the promises and oaths you did swear before the altar of St Peter.

According to the chronicle, William fell prostrate before the venerable prophetic figure, begging to be told his offences so that he might offer restitution. Again, it is the humility of the King that strains our credulity, not the recitation of his wrongdoing. William's rapacity and cruelty form the common backdrop to most of the events recorded in the early histories.

The oppressive character of the Norman regime was firmly established in 1069-70. It was intensified by the resistance of those English leaders, in Church and State, who caused the invaders so much trouble. Whether the outcome would have been any different in the long run if the native earls, thegns and abbots had bowed their necks submissively beneath the alien yoke we cannot know, but it is clear that with every drop of Norman blood spilled and every castle attacked William's attitude hardened. He may have originally intended to disturb the political and social status quo as little as possible in order to win the support of the ruling class, but he ended up reallocating virtually all the land to his own followers, appointing Norman ecclesiastics to all the top Church jobs and treating the English contemptuously as a conquered and inferior race.

The chronicles, written by scribes in monastic scriptoria, tell us a great deal about the fate of the English landholding class and even more about the indignities suffered by churchmen. They are as indifferent as the invaders to the lives of the common people. But it takes little reading between the lines to discover something of the sufferings of those who asked of life only a roof over their heads and food in their stomachs. Thousands died because of the fighting. Tens of thousands more from the famine which resulted from their standing crops being torched and their livestock confiscated. Add to these the people driven from their burning, looted homes and you gain some concept of the devastation visited upon many parts of the country. Images come to mind of the columns of stumbling, ragged, fear-haunted refugees fleeing before the Nazi occupiers of central and western Europe in 1940-41.

Yet, in some ways worse must have been the psychological impact of the occupation. The native population was mentally cowed by the arrogance of the invaders, an arrogance bred of

William I was hugely successful in everything he undertook in an age where 'success' was almost synonymous with 'ruthlessness'.

military superiority. The Normans boasted a war machine second to none in eleventh-century Europe. Just as the countries overrun by Germany in the opening campaigns of World War II had no answer to panzer divisions and Luftwaffe squadrons, so the English and their allies were not equipped to face Norman military tactics based on heavy cavalry and castles. Both innovations had been refined in northern France as means of dealing with Viking raids. Armoured knights charging en masse were an effective answer to axe-wielding foot soldiers. Castles provided both defensive and offensive potential. Soldiers and local residents could retire within their walls at the onset of a raid and use them as bases for counter-attack. English military leaders had no understanding of this new technology. On the rare occasions when they captured a castle (as at York), they destroyed it, rather than turn it to their own use.

These strange phenomena were overwhelming. The knight on his high horse and the motte and bailey that towered over the countryside represented in a very physical way the dominance and the domineering nature of the new rulers. They literally looked down on the English. The first action of king or tenant-in-chief in subduing an area was to build a castle, which served as a garrison HQ and also an administrative centre from which to rule his subjects. The strange, oppressive buildings sprang up like mushrooms everywhere. Or, rather, they did not spring up; the local people were drafted into work gangs to build them, to dig the ditches and erect the wooden towers which were to be the landmarks of Norman oppression. It was hard work, particularly if the taskmasters were in a hurry. A new castle could be finished in as little as eight days. It did not help the aching labourers to know that they were creating their own chains of bondage. The Normans' military power gave them the illusion of cultural superiority. The customs of these medieval Herrenvolk were different. They spoke French, the language of the 'civilised' European upper classes. Soon they would be studding the landscape with Romanesque buildings. England became a country of two peoples – a Norman aristocracy and an English underclass.

In 1069 Archbishop Aldred ordered loads of food to be brought into York for the celebration of a church feast. The sheriff, William Mallet, chanced upon the loaded wagons and demanded to know where all this produce was headed. On being told that it was for the church, he ordered the Archbishop's men to convey it, instead, to the castle for the pleasure of himself and his knights. Such events symbolise the arrogance and contempt of the conquerors and the helpless resentment of the conquered. In the early days of the regime change, Englishmen allowed themselves to hope that Norman rule would be of short duration. The events of 1069-70 dashed any such hope.

What Happened Before...

1349   ROTTENEST YEAR

... And What Came After

1349

Parsons and parish priests begged the bishop, because their parishes were so poor since the pestilence time, to give them licence to live in London and sing for simony. Silver is sweet!

The Vision of Piers Plowman

A FEW YEARS after the 'Pestilence' – the pandemic known to later ages as the Black Death – a Malvern man named William Langland wrote a long allegorical poem, *The Vision of Piers Plowman*, in which he pointed out the miseries of ordinary working people, the failures of those in power and, particularly, the shortcomings of the clergy. The picture Langland presented of mid-fourteenth-century England was bleak. It was a country not so much suffering from depopulation and physical ills as in the grip of a deep moral and spiritual malaise. As the quotation above indicates, Langland reserved his severest criticism for parish clergy, who in the aftermath of the Black Death tried to benefit from the shortage of priests by abandoning the poor people in the country to go and sing masses in the city for the souls of the wealthy departed. Nothing tells us more about the state of a society than how those in charge behave in a time of crisis.

Morbidly hued stories about the Black Death locate its first traceable origins in the Crimea, where infected Mongol invaders were besieging the city of Caffa in 1346-7. After some months, frustrated by the endurance of the inhabitants, the attackers took to catapulting dead bodies over the walls. Soon there were piles of rotting carcases piling up in the streets. Citizens were afraid to bury them in case they caught the horrible disease that had killed them. But that disease, whatever it was, spread anyway. Before long, panic set in. Merchants and any others who could get passage thronged the harbour and crowded onto ships to avoid the contagion. By the autumn of 1347, several fugitives from the Crimea arrived in Sicily – or, rather, the ships carrying them arrived. Some of the vessels were manned by skeleton crews of dying men. Others drifted onshore, their decks strewn with corpses. Opportunist Sicilians grabbed the chance to help themselves to the cargoes and brought ashore more than they had expected.

The plague propagated itself with astonishing alacrity. Within days it was galloping along Europe's busy trade routes. The responsibility for its arrival in the British Isles is claimed by Weymouth. A harbourside plaque announces:

THE "BLACK DEATH" ENTERED ENGLAND IN 1348
THROUGH THIS PORT.
***
IT KILLED 30-50% OF THE COUNTRY'S TOTAL
POPULATION.

Other traditions name Bristol as the place of entry. In all probability there was no one port through which those carrying the plague bacillus exclusively arrived but the disease certainly spread eastwards and northwards from south-west England. By the autumn of 1348 it had reached the crowded wen of London, England's social and commercial hub. There was no stopping it now.

But what exactly was this terrible scourge? Experts disagree in their diagnoses. For years it was accepted that the culprit was the bacterium *Yersinia pestis*, carried by the fleas of the black rat (*Rattus rattus*). *Y. pestis* is a form of bubonic plague that has broken out several times in world history and is named after its main symptom, the swellings or buboes which appear in the groins and armpits of sufferers. The problem with this explanation is that bubonic plague is not sufficiently contagious to account for the phenomenally rapid spread of disease. A much more virulent strain is pneumonic plague, which affects the lungs and can be transmitted through the air by coughs and sneezes. But some modern theories propose other possible culprits, such as a strain of the ebola virus, which transmits itself rapidly from person to person in unsanitary conditions, and anthrax, which travels easily between humans and animals. Descriptions of the Pestilence's symptoms vary and, of course, lack the precision of 21st-century clinical diagnosis. It may even be that the fourteenth-century pandemic involved more than one disease. Whatever the truth, the Pestilence raged fiercely throughout 1349 and only began to subside the following year. Accounts of those who experienced the epidemic and lived at least long enough to record what they saw make heart-rending reading:

...the grievous plague... came to Bristol and it was as if all the strength of the town had died, as if they had been hit with sudden death, for their were few who stayed in their beds more than three days, or two days, or even one half a day...

...this cruel death spread on all sides, following the course of the sun. And there died at Leicester, in the small parish of Holy Cross, 400; in the parish of St Margaret's, Leicester, 700; and so in every parish.

...in the kingdom of Scotland... to such a pitch did the plague wreak its cruel spite that nearly a third of mankind were made to pay the debt of nature. Moreover, by God's will, this evil led to a strange and unwonted kind of death, insomuch that the flesh of the sick was sometimes puffed out and swollen, and they dragged out their earthly life for barely two days.

...the dead were left in fields and lanes, their bodies so corrupted by the plague that neither beast nor bird would touch them.

In Wales death came... into our midst like black smoke, a plague which cuts off the young, a rootless phantom which has no mercy for fair countenance. Woe is me of the shilling in the armpit! It is seething, terrible... a head that gives pain and causes a loud cry... great is its seething like a burning cinder...

The plague was so contagious that those touching the dead or even the sick were immediately infected and died and the one confessing and the confessor were together led to the grave... some died as if in a frenzy, from pain of the head, others from spitting blood...The cities of Dublin and Drogheda were almost destroyed and wasted of inhabitants... in Dublin alone from the beginning of August right up to Christmas fourteen thousand men died... There was scarcely a house in which only one died but commonly man and wife with their children and family going one way, namely crossing to death.

The most extensive description of the Pestilence was penned by the contemporary Italian writer, Giovanni Boccaccio. In the introduction to his collection of ribald stories, *The Decameron*, he described the impact of multiple deaths on the people of Florence and Tuscany. There is no reason to suppose that the reactions of their British counterparts were any different.

Whenever people died, their neighbours always followed a single, set routine, prompted as much by their fear of being contaminated by the decaying corpse as by any charitable feelings they may have entertained towards the deceased... they extracted the bodies of the dead from their houses and left them lying outside their front doors... Funeral biers would be sent for, upon which the dead were taken away, though there were some who, for lack of biers, were carried off on plain boards. It was by no means rare for one of these biers to be seen with two or three bodies on it at a time; on the contrary, many were seen to contain a husband and wife, two or three brothers and sisters, a father and son, or some other pair of close relatives... there were no tears or candles or mourners to honour the dead; in fact, no more respect was recorded to dead people than would nowadays be shown to dead goats... the one thing which, in normal times, no wise man had ever learned to accept with patient resignation… had now been brought home to the feeble-minded as well, but the scale of the calamity caused them to regard it with indifference.

This reads like the medieval equivalent of compassion fatigue. In London the authorities initially created new cemeteries to cope with the emergency but these were so rapidly filled that the attempt to keep pace with the number of burials had to be abandoned. Recent excavations in Smithfield have disclosed that bodies were stacked five deep in mass graves. This was more likely to be the rule than the exception in centres of high density population.

A sufferer instructed to strap a live hen to the swelling in his armpit or drink a daily pint of his own urine might, at least, have his hopes raised.

The first reaction of terrified people in neighbourhoods where the plague broke out was to flee. Which, of course, only assisted the spread of the disease. By the end of 1349 the Pestilence had reached all parts of mainland Britain and crossed to Ireland. Ironically, the Scots hastened their own downfall. Smarting at their recent thrashing by an English army at the Battle of Neville's Cross and the capture of their King, David II, they took advantage of their neighbour's weakened state to cross the border in force. Whatever booty they returned with was bought at an appalling price, for the contagion went with it.

The paradox at the heart of the Black Death is that it changed very little and, yet, changed everything. The material knock-on effects of mass deaths were immediate and obvious to all. Unharvested crops rotted in the fields. When the loaded grain wagons stopped rolling, the mills fell silent. Bread was in short supply, so its price escalated. Unfed animals lay moaning in their byres, unless opportunist neighbours appropriated them. When the homes of the wealthy lay open and unguarded by their owner's retainers, looters were soon at work, prepared to risk contagion for the sake of a quick buck. The inability of the law courts to sit regularly was an open invitation to all kinds of crime. Medieval economies were delicately balanced at the best of times. They certainly could not cope with disruption on the scale of that caused by the Black Death. Agriculture and trade languished and that meant that rents, taxes and duties did not get paid. Cornish tin mining came to a virtual halt. Because tin was mixed with silver to make the pennies that were the basis of the currency, this meant that the government could not mint enough new coins to sustain its own expenditure and the commercial life of the kingdom. Foreign trade hit the doldrums because of a shortage of fit and healthy mariners to work the ships and also because ports were closed for fear of the Pestilence.

There were also long-term changes. The pandemic threatened to turn the social pyramid upside down. The basis of the rural economy was villeinage, that is, a peasantry tied to the land who tilled their own holdings in return for service to the lord of the manor. It was an ancient system, hallowed by centuries of tradit`ion, and had the fundamental advantage of maintaining social stability. Families stayed put for generations and had no incentive to move. It was, of course, a system that worked well for the upper class and it operated like clockwork as long as there was a buoyant labour market. Now, suddenly, there was a dire shortage of

husbandmen, herdsmen and shepherds. Agricultural workers could sell their services to the highest bidder. And there
was no lack of bidders. Landlords desperate to have their
fields and flocks properly managed had no alternative but to
pay men to work for them. In 1347 a ploughman's wage was
two shillings a week. By 1350 he could demand – and get –
ten shillings a week for his labour. At the same time commodity prices dropped, due to decreasing demand. The
ecclesiastical chronicler, Henry Knighton of Leicester,
recorded:

> There were small prices for virtually everything. A man
> could have a horse, which was worth 40 shillings, for 6 shil-
> lings and 8 pence, a cow for 12 pence... Sheep and cattle
> were wandering over fields and through crops, and there
> was no-one to drive or gather them together.

For those occupying the upper strata of feudal society,
whose income depended ultimately on agricultural produce
– nobles, bishops, abbots, knights of the shire – the economic
upheaval was disastrous. They had no alternative but to
compete in the labour market, offering high wages, incen-
tives such as free food and drink and other fringe benefits.
Some landowners lost out in the competition for labour
and staved off bankruptcy by selling off chunks of their
estates. It was ecclesiastical landlords who tended to hold
out most stubbornly. St Edmundsbury Abbey in Suffolk was
one of the richest in Europe and its abbot believed that
he was in a position to resist change. Resist it he did but from
that time the monastery went into a steady decline. Those
who benefited from the collapse of land values were enterprising peasants who were able to cobble together enough

cash to get themselves started as small-time landlords. A thrusting 'peasant aristocracy', the yeoman farmers, emerged, elbowing their way into the respectable, property-owning echelons of society. Those unable to raise the necessary finance found other ways to 'better' themselves by moving into the towns and setting up as general labourers or craftsmen.

It is easy for us to gather documentary evidence and identify such long-term trends but, of course, for fourteenth-century men and women, change was more difficult to recognise. The concept of the free market economy was totally alien to the medieval mind and these first, tentative steps towards it certainly did not change attitudes overnight – or even over-century. The hierarchic nature of society was accepted as a given and its authentication – or, at least, its justification – was provided by the Church. Just as in the heavenly realm there were descending ranks of archangels, angels, saints and martyrs, so among men God had appointed a hallowed order: pope, emperor, kings, nobles, gentlemen and so on down to the landless serf. Governments were always sensitive to anything that threatened to shake the established framework. To them it was treason. To the Church it was sin. The social order was static and must be maintained. But while they clung to established beliefs and values, the leaders of society could not avoid the fact that the plague had introduced a new dynamism into human relationships. Just as the disease itself defied diagnosis and treatment, so its social impact was uncontrollable. There was nothing either politicians or theologians could do to stop it. The crisis played havoc with traditional beliefs. For example, according to religious doctrine, absolution was the sole prerogative of the priesthood. But priests were now in short supply. Was one doomed to die unshriven because no religious functionary could get to one's deathbed in time? The Bishop of Bath and Wells addressed himself to this problem as early as January 1349:

> Since no priests can be found who are willing, whether out of zeal or devotion to… take pastoral care of the aforesaid places, nor to visit the sick and administer to them the sacraments of the church, we understand that many people are dying without the sacrament of penance. [Therefore]… persuade all men, in particular those who are now sick or should feel sick in the future, that, if they are on the point of death and cannot secure the services of a priest, then they should make confession to each other… or, if no man is present, then even to a woman[!]

This solution undermined the concept of the priest's unique sacerdotal nature that defined his very place within the social order. Yet few people drew the logical conclusions stemming from such developments. To most contemporaries the kinds of changes I have been referring to must have seemed merely like necessary adjustments. No-one thought in terms of society being revolutionised. This is what I mean when I suggest that the Pestilence changed little but changed everything.

What everyone longed to do – what people going through a traumatic crisis always want to do – was get back to normal. And, superficially, that is what happened – remarkably quickly. Britain had become over-populated by the 1340s. That is to say that, in several parts of the country, the land could not provide work enough or food enough for all the people. The results were increasing poverty, vagabondage and crime. To that extent the plague provided a necessary, if appalling, 'final solution'. The survivors were able to extract a better living from their holdings. Although villages and some small towns disappeared from the map, the reverse of the coin was a more sustainable husbandry, much of it in the hands of new owners or tenants. As long as there were workers eager to step into dead men's shoes, the pattern of springtime and harvest could continue. Landowners found themselves on the wrong side of the bargaining balance but, as long as they were able and willing to pay increased wages and lease out holdings on more attractive terms, they were able to stay in business.

In the meantime, the leaders of society made futile attempts to reverse the process of social and economic change. The King issued the Ordinance of Labourers (1349), which decreed that wages were to be pegged at pre-plague rates. He might just as well have ordered the waves of the sea to stop advancing up the beach.

New sumptuary laws were introduced, even some dictating what people were allowed to wear. Dress was an indicator of social status, so, when nouveau-riche peasants began to don furs and silks, it signified to their superiors that the world had turned on its head. Before the plague came, only the richest in the land were permitted to wear furs. Afterwards, new laws, grudgingly making concessions to the inevitable, tried to dictate who should wear what: white stoat (ermine) fur for nobles and gentlemen with an annual income above £266 p.a.; merchants and artisans, even if they were richer than that, had to be content with lambskin; those lower down the social scale might only adorn themselves with rabbit or cat fur. In fact, people wore whatever they could afford.

It may seem strange, even shocking, that the government's main concern when faced with this tragedy was the maintenance of social distinctions. If a major epidemic struck Britain today a state of national emergency would be declared. Relief services would be deployed from central and regional depots to provide medical aid to the sick, distribute food to survivors and arrange for the efficient disposal of bodies. But, as the novelist L.P. Hartley observed, 'The past is a foreign country: they do things differently there.' Society was rigidly stratified. For one thing, natural disasters were considered to be visitations of divine judgement. Banishing the plague was, therefore, a matter of prayer and repentance – the responsibility of the Church (which made the desertion of many parish clergy even more heinous). It was also the case that King and court were remote from the mass of the people and concerned themselves with matters more important, in their eyes, than massive depopulation.

King Edward III, now in his mid-thirties, was a vigorous, athletic warrior-king at the height of his powers – and had devoted the greater part of his energies during his reign so far to trying to extend his rule over France and France's ally, Scotland. For him war was royal; war was glorious; war was what kings did. But his attempt to claim the crown of France had thrown England into an intermittent conflict which would far outlive the King himself, one known as the Hundred Years War. And to pay for his foreign adventures Edward had already borrowed heavily on the international money markets (his Italian bankers went bust when he

THE ORDER OF THE GARTER

The Order of the Garter was a new community of chivalry – chivalry being an attempt to clothe with romance and honour the sordid business of bashing heads and burning down peasant homes. The Garter and similar orders founded by other monarchs were meant to parallel monasticism. Just as monks donned hair shirts, fasted and denied themselves creature comforts to prove their otherworldly holiness, so knights undertook extravagant displays of loyalty to king, country and the god of battles. Some were just plain silly, like the custom adopted by mounted 'heroes' of covering one eye with a patch (in some cases, both eyes!) until they had proved themselves in combat. Orders of chivalry set their members apart from 'ordinary' people as clearly as the monastic vocation separated the cowled brotherhoods from mere lay folk. And when they were not riding off to war, these gorgeously caparisoned thugs competed with one another in the highly ritualised contests of the tiltyard.

According to later tradition the Garter emblem and motto originated in a trivial event. The King supposedly retrieved the garter dropped by a lady of the court and silenced his sniggering attendants with the words 'Honi soit qui mal y pense' - 'Shame to him who thinks ill of it'. However Edward's aims were probably specifically political. The colours of the Garter emblem – blue and gold – were those of the arms of France and the motto almost certainly urged members not to be ashamed of Edward's claim to the French crown.

defaulted on payments in 1341) and taxed his subjects to the hilt.

When the Pestilence struck England in 1348, Edward's reputation was actually riding high. A phenomenally successful campaign in France in 1347 had culminated in him inflicting a crushing defeat on the French King, Philip VI, at Crécy-en-Ponthieu. Edward had then gone on to capture the well-defended port of Calais (which remained in English hands for over 200 years). The pickings of this campaign had been vast. The English army had plundered and looted its way through Normandy. It was said that the soldiers had returned with so much booty that no woman in the realm had lacked for some graceful gown or valuable trinket.

On his return from France, Edward entered on a round of lavish and expensive celebrations. He added new buildings to Windsor Castle and, when all was ready, either in April 1348 or 1349, he made it the centre of a warrior fellowship modelled on that of the legendary King Arthur. He, too, he decided, would have a round table where his knights would feast and plan heroic exploits. He formed his chosen companions into a new community of chivalry, the exclusive Order of the Garter.

It was not possible for Edward to be completely oblivious to the sufferings of tens of thousands of his subjects, but his conduct displayed a distinct arrogant insouciance. There is no evidence of him instituting relief measures or even expressing sympathy for the afflicted. Such initiatives as he did take had more to do with minimising inconvenience to himself and the governing class than alleviating the hardships of the majority. The Ordinance of Labourers was intended to protect the landowning class from the economic effects of the plague and betrayed no understanding of the labour market. Two years later, the government was still ordering workers to return to their masters on pain of punishment. Edward's response to the deplorable state of London's streets was to draw the mayor's attention to their disgusting condition. The King was right. With its thoroughfares choked with bodies and human and animal filth, the capital resembled a badly supervised sewer. But it was hardly helpful simply to order the city fathers to restore the pre-plague situation. The mayor and his colleagues would willingly have complied if they could have found any labourers in the depopulated square mile to undertake the necessary clean-up. It was all they could do to cope with the complex horrors of a disease that would eventually carry off 30,000 of the capital's citizens. In some instances, the King actually turned the Pestilence to his own advantage. It provided him with an excellent excuse to prorogue the parliament of 1349, which was proving particularly troublesome. And, at a time when landowners were being forced to pay higher wages, Edward increased the rents levied upon holders of Crown lands in order to prevent himself being affected by the economic meltdown.

The King could be aloof because the pandemic did not come very close to him. Boccaccio recorded that 'many valiant men and fair ladies breakfasted with their kinsfolk and supped with their ancestors in paradise'. The Pestilence was certainly no respecter of persons but, inevitably, it was at its most virulent in the crowded, unsanitary streets of Britain's towns and the rural hovels where human families shared their living space with vermin. The King and the beautiful people of his court seldom exposed themselves to the sights and smells of the dwellings of 'mere' subjects. They retired to their castles and spacious country dwellings where they could (literally and metaphorically) pull up the drawbridge connecting them with the disease-ridden world. They were as oblivious to suffering humanity as most of us are to the impact of HIV/Aids in sub-Saharan Africa. The only personal tragedy Edward suffered was the death of Joan, one of his five daughters, but she contacted the plague well away from home, in Bordeaux, when she was on her way to be married to a Castilian prince. The King got off lightly; the rich and powerful usually do. But his people were not stupid. They noted the indifference of their monarch and his haughty courtiers, and the gap between ruler and ruled was irrevocably widened by the Black Death, although it would be a generation before discord would erupt in the Peasants' Revolt (1381).

The most important immediate effects of the Pestilence were psychological. Just as deep personal tragedy leaves permanent mental scars in the life of the sufferer, so communities, neighbourhoods and nations are marked by major disasters. We know this in our own age. The last century has seen Britain involved in many wars but the conflict of 1914-18 occupies a special place in the national psyche. The carnage in the muddy fields of Flanders has become a powerful icon of the futility and horror of war. And in medieval Britain, people responded to the Pestilence in a variety of ways. Once again it is Boccaccio who summarises the reactions most eloquently. One of his characters urges flight from Florence and the futility of remaining in the city:

...if we go out of doors we shall see the dead and the sick

being carried hither and thither or we shall see people once condemned to exile by the courts for their misdeeds careering wildly about the streets in open defiance of the law, well knowing that those appointed to enforce it are either dead or dying; or else we shall find ourselves at the mercy of the scum of the city who… go prancing and bustling all over the place, singing bawdy songs that add insult to our injuries… And if we return to our homes what happens?… Wherever I go in the house, wherever I pause to rest, I seem to be haunted by the shades of the departed, whose faces no longer appear as I remember them but with strange and horribly twisted expressions that frighten me out of my senses.

Grief and a sense of helplessness pervaded the land. These emotions affected the work of dramatists, musicians and painters. A common theme taken up by artists from this time was the *danse macabre*, the dance of death, which represented prancing skeletons gleefully claiming men and women irrespective of social standing.

When people experience personal tragedy their first anguished reaction is often to scream, 'Why?' 'Why me?' 'Why us?' By far the commonest answer available, in an age which viewed God as a meter out of rewards and punishments was: 'Because of your sins'. And indeed, at the time, popular preachers (or, at least, those who stayed at their posts) urged self-examination and public penance. To many it seemed that this visitation by *Pestilence*, one of the four horsemen of the Apocalypse, could only presage the end of the world. In several parts of Europe hysteria drove some frightened zealots to alarming extremes of behaviour. Groups of men and women, known as *flagellantes*, went from town to town, lashing themselves with whips as a dramatic expression of contrition. Mobs seeking scapegoats readily turned on the Jews (always the 'usual suspects' when any kind of disaster struck) and carried out unspeakable cruelties of fresh persecution. In some places even cat hunts were instigated, in the belief that cats were the devil's familiars. Removing these natural predators of mice and rats, of course, only made matters worse. Other no less frantic groups followed an opposite regimen. According to Boccaccio, they

> maintained that an infallible way of warding off this appalling evil was to drink heavily, enjoy life to the full, go around singing and merrymaking, gratify all of one's cravings whenever the opportunity offered and shrug the whole thing off as an enormous joke.

Astrologers offered an alternative reason for the pandemic. According to these watchers of the skies, the culprits were Saturn, Jupiter and Mars. These planets had found themselves conjoined in the sign of Aquarius, the originator of 'moist humours', and this had induced the earth to emit poisonous vapours. The appropriate treatment, according to the magi, had nothing to do with appeasing an angry God by masochistic excesses, seeking oblivion in the bottle, or taking out one's own anger on helpless victims. A much more philosophical regime was recommended: the sufferer should avoid eating poultry, waterfowl, pork, or 'old beef'. To eat fish was to court disaster, as was the use of rainwater in the preparation of meals. Exercise should be taken only in moderation and on no account whatsoever

'WITCHES, WIZARDS AND CUNNING MEN HAD IN THEIR REPER-
TOIRE AN INFINITE STORE OF SPELLS, POTIONS AND PRACTICES
TO PROPOSE TO THE AFFLICTED...'

should one take a bath. The patient should develop inner calm. He should not reflect on death or anything else distressing. Let him rather direct his meditations to:

> pleasing, agreeable and delicious things... Beautiful landscapes and fine gardens should be visited, particularly when aromatic plants are flowering... Listening to beautiful, melodious songs is wholesome and the contemplation of gold, silver and precious stones is comforting to the heart.

Hardly the most practical advice for the peasant family huddled together fearfully in their damp cottage, with never a ruby or amethyst in sight.

What of the medical profession? Did fourteenth-century doctors have any useful nostrums to offer to the few sufferers who could afford their fees? The very appearance of a plague physician was designed to terrify rather than reassure the patient. He would arrive clad shoulder to toe in a black topcoat, his head covered with a wide-brimmed hat. His face was hidden behind a mask with red glass eyepieces from which protruded an eagle-like beak. This was, in reality, a container for aromatic herbs and spices that were thought to counteract the contaminated air of the sick room.

If the patient survived the shock of the doctor's appearance, he had to submit to a variety of treatments, which, as we now know, were totally ineffective. His buboes would be lanced, supposedly to let the infection out. That done, the incisions would be smeared with a poultice of human excrement and pounded lily root, bound with tree resin. The next part of the treatment was the physicians' standby – bleeding. Veins would be opened to draw off 'infected' blood, a practice that can have done nothing to strengthen the patient's constitution. Before departing, the doctor might leave a medicine to be taken regularly, a composition of powdered eggshells, chopped marigold leaves and treacle mixed with mulled ale. That, at least, cannot have done much harm.

The vast majority of people turned to local 'practitioners' of beneficent magic. Witches, wizards and cunning men had in their repertoire an infinite store of spells, potions and practices to propose to the afflicted, and one is tempted to think that the more bizarre the treatments on offer, the more likely patients were to believe in their efficacy. A sufferer instructed to strap a live hen to the swelling in his armpit or drink a daily pint of his own urine might, at least, have his hopes raised and, such is the nature of human credulity, that the inevitable failure of the treatment seldom affected the local reputation of the sorcerer.

The important fact is that there was no salvation. Nothing worked. No-one could help. With very few exceptions, anyone smitten with the plague died, and died in agony. The only good thing that could be said for the Pestilence was that it killed quickly – in days, or even hours. Britain, in common with a large part of the known world, was in the grip of something as incomprehensible as it was deadly. As far as extant records reveal, it seems that Britain largely avoided the manifestations of exaggerated frenzy and violence that were common on the continent. Processions of bleeding, wailing flagellants were not seen on the streets of London or Bristol. Since the last Jews had been expelled from England two generations earlier, the nation was spared the experiments in mass extermination that occurred elsewhere. But that is not to say that the distress, anxiety and bewilderment underlying such macabre asceticism and inhuman persecution were not shared by British men and women. In psychological terms this visitation of plague was, truly, a *Black* Death.

What really made the plague year one of the worst in our history was the growing realisation that no-one had an answer to the desperate questions the Black Death posed. Not the Church. Not the medical profession. Not the rulers of the nation at central or local level. Every individual sufferer was alone with his pain. Every bereaved parent and child alone with his/her grief. Most victims who died went into the blackness of eternity without the comfort of a sustaining faith and the appropriate rite of passage. The ancient beliefs and convictions that had held society together no longer carried credibility. Traditional social ties were weakened. Crime increased. In a land where life was cheap, the annual rate of homicides doubled. The nation's moral joints were loosened as people abandoned their mutual responsibilities and pursued their own ends as best they could. The twentieth century witnessed something similar. The hammer blows of tragedy that struck Western society between 1914 and 1945 changed forever, not only political and economic structures, but the assumptions which provided the cement of those structures – traditional Christianity, the class system, the confident belief in white superiority. Then it was issues such as carnage on the western front, unemployment, poor living conditions and depressed wage levels that alienated people from their leaders; but the prevailing mood of hopelessness, resentment and fear links the two epochs.

The Black Death did not create the tensions in society; it exposed the tensions that already existed. When the worst tragedy in living memory struck, the world fractured at its weak points. It was the strongest part of the structure which turned out to be the most vulnerable. The Church was a reactionary monolith that exercised power over people by its claimed control of their eternal destiny. Villagers were obliged to pay a tenth of the annual yield from their fields to the clergy because they were told that, if they and their departed loved ones were ever to reach heaven, they needed the prayers, sacraments and rituals which only the clergy could provide. That was all very well when priests, monks and higher clergy demonstrably lived lives in accord with their holy calling. But many did not. And their worldliness and corruption had long since provoked criticism:

You pope-holy priests, full of presumption
With your wide furred hoods void of discretion
Unto your own preaching of contrary condition
Which causes the people to have less devotion.
Whoever [takes] a benefice for richness and ease
Should [be made to serve] his living in [a place of] sickness
Rather than serve God as he pleases.

However bad harvests were or however stricken animals were with disease, peasants still had to trundle off with their wagons of produce to the monastic tithe barns for the benefit of inmates who were strangers to the back-breaking labour of tilling, hoeing and reaping. William Langland attacked the higher clergy who lived like lords on their vast estates:

…take their land from them, you nobles, and let them live on their tithes! For surely, if property is a deadly poison that corrupts them, it would be good for Holy Church's sake to relieve them of it and purge them of the poison before it grows more dangerous…

Anticlericalism had hovered not far below the surface of everyday life for a number of years by the time the plague struck. As recently as 1327, 3,000 armed townsmen had broken into the abbey of St Edmundsbury, destroyed the sacristy, rifled the treasury, looted precious objects and documents, flogged the monks and forced the abbot to agree to a charter of liberties granting the town virtual independence (a block and headsman's axe were set before him to help him make up his mind). However, it was the failure of many clergy to remain at their posts during the pandemic that revealed the hollowness of their profession. It has been estimated that in cities such as York and Lincoln twenty per cent of the parish priests fled, and these places were not atypical. Thus, not only could the clergy not explain why the plague had come or offer practical help to the afflicted, many of them also reneged on their spiritual duties. And matters became worse in the immediate aftermath of the Pestilence, for, to make up for the numbers of priests who died, bishops hastened to ordain virtually any man who offered himself. Thus, the quality of the Church's personnel actually declined.

The final verdict on 1349 can be summed up in the words 'loss of faith'. As one poet gloomily observed:

God is deaf nowadays and deigneth not hear us,
And prayers have no power the plague to stay.

Belief in the country's secular and religious leadership was shaken. People did not stop being loyal or patriotic or Christian but they were much more likely to question exactly what 'loyalty', 'patriotism' and 'Christianity' meant. In the long term, free-thinking produced a sea change of national attitudes. Political and religious challenge became more frequent. By the century's end, the Peasants' Revolt had broken out and England had produced its own native-grown heresy, Wycliffism. But such developments were a long way off when an Irish chronicler recorded:

I, as if among the dead, waiting till death do come, have put into writing truthfully what I have heard and verified. And, so that the writing may not perish with the scribe... I have added parchment to continue it, if, by any chance, anyone may be left in the future and any child of Adam may escape this pestilence and continue the work thus commenced.

At this point another hand-wrote the words 'Here it seems that the author died'.

What Happened Before...

1536   ROTTENEST YEAR

...And What Came After

1536

IT'S OFFICIAL, THE GOVERNMENT IS SET TO NATIONALISE FOOTBALL

SPEAKING AT A NEWS conference this morning the Sports Minister, Brian Tooley, outlined plans for what he called 'a long overdue clean-up of the national game'.

Flanked by the Deputy Prime Minister and the veteran moral campaigner, Vic Young, Tooley listed the vices:

1. Too many clubs in foreign ownership.
2. The preponderance of overseas players.
3. Fat cat managers 'dealing' in players for 'obscene' fees.
4. Player salaries which have gone 'through the roof'.
5. Loutish off-the-field behaviour which sets an appalling example to our young people.

'The F.A. has had plenty of time to put its house in order,' the minister said. 'Their failure leaves the government no choice but to intervene.' With immediate effect all lower division teams are to be taken into public ownership. All foreign players to be repatriated when their contracts expire. Transfer fees and salaries to be capped. 'And the writing is on the wall for the major league clubs,' the minister said. 'If they don't get the message and reform themselves, they, too, will face takeover.' He estimated that £1 billion in club assets would be freed up by these measures. 'We will use the money to fund the government's "sport for all" programme,' he said.

Pressed to comment on the rumour that he also intended to overhaul the rules of the game, Tooley confirmed that the new Football Council would have a wide remit. 'We rule nothing in and nothing out to restore the healthy image of this great sport,' he said.

Given that football is the closest thing Britain now has to a national religion, the backlash that would undoubtedly ensue from such a draconian government initiative gives a fair indication of the shockwave that ran through the country when, in 1536, Henry VIII took over the English Church and set about asset stripping.

Back in 1509, 27 years earlier, the reign had all started so well. The tall, extrovert, athletic Henry VIII had come to the throne when he was just short of his eighteenth birthday. He had immediately married the widow of his deceased elder brother, the Spanish Princess, Catherine of Aragon. He was handsome and athletic. She was pretty and vivacious. They were an ideal royal couple, presiding over a court thronged with beautiful people. They were the Posh and Becks of the age – fashion icons for the aspiring men and women of the upper classes and idolised by the people at large.

They had an efficient PR machine. Every summer they went on progress through the shires closest to London, and villagers turned out to cheer the glittering royal cavalcade as it passed or to watch Henry and his companions as they went hunting. In the rest of the year, when the court was usually established at Richmond or Greenwich, close to the capital, Henry frequently put on tournaments and water pageants for the enjoyment of the people and the enhancement of his image. The dreary business of everyday politics was largely left to the King's ministers, primarily Thomas Wolsey, who held the most important offices in both Church and State and who became a cardinal in 1515.

The party went on for a decade or more. But the good times were not destined to roll for ever. Various problems beset the young couple and undermined their relationship,

> **Cromwell's agents confiscated numerous objects of superstition... They included the chains with which St Peter was bound, the coals over which St Laurence was roasted, St Edmund's toe-nail clippings and enough fragments of the true cross to make a whole new one and still leave some over.**

the most serious being Catherine's inability to produce a male heir to the throne, which, as Queen, was her principal duty. A run of miscarriages and cot deaths transformed the lithe bride of 1509 into a dumpy, prematurely middle-aged woman with only one surviving daughter to show for her succession of confinements. Henry, who was always genuinely religious, struggled to find an answer to the question why God seemed to have deserted the Tudor dynasty, thus making the succession insecure and threatening England with a return to the baronial rivalries of the Wars of the Roses. He finally concluded that he had been wrong to take Catherine to wife in the first place. His marriage within the Church's prohibited degrees had needed a papal dispensation but, as he now convinced himself, such a union was forbidden by the Bible and not even a pope could get round the divine prohibition.

Henry was not the only person to be questioning the authority of Rome. Throughout the 1520s criticism of the papacy had been gathering momentum. The protest of a German monk, Martin Luther, at certain corrupt ecclesiastical practices had struck a common chord with men and women throughout Latin Christendom. The Reformation he launched spread with amazing rapidity because it expressed the doubts thousands had experienced but feared to speak. Soon many of Henry's subjects, from simple tradesmen to free-thinking clergy and even members of the royal court, were excited adherents of the new ideas. The King was not one of them but his own circumstances made him sympathetic to the rising clamour for religious reform.

A conventional Christian believer, Henry had become convinced that his dynastic problem was God's punishment for the sinful marriage he had contracted. Accordingly, he had asked the Pope to grant him an annulment, which he refused to do. This created a dilemma for the King. He regarded himself as an orthodox Catholic but his own problems were edging him closer towards the religious radicals. God, Henry was convinced, could not want to see the collapse of the Tudor dynasty, which would plunge England back into the civil conflict (the Wars of the Roses) from which Henry VII had delivered it in 1485. Therefore, the Pope must be defying the will of God. By the late 1520s the situation had become complicated (or, in Henry's eyes, simplified) by the fact that he had fallen in love with Anne Boleyn, a woman of the court some sixteen years his junior. There was no doubt in the King's mind that with Anne he would sire a whole nursery full of princes. The more Rome stalled over the annulment issue, the more determined Henry became to have his own way.

There seemed no prospect of escaping the impasse. Wolsey could offer no solution and so Henry dumped him. It was Thomas Cromwell, the minister who succeeded the cardinal, who came up with the draconian answer. This was to dispense with the Pope and make a unilateral declaration of England's independence from Rome. In 1531 Henry was recognised by parliament as Supreme Head of the Church in England. Within two years the King's marriage to Catherine was annulled by the new Archbishop of Canterbury, Thomas Cranmer, and Henry had married Anne Boleyn.

That could have been the end of a distressing and disturbing period in the life of the King and the kingdom. It turned out to be just the beginning. England had become the first major power to cut itself adrift from the Roman Church. It was a momentous step and eager reformers, thrilled to have got away with it, looked forward to even more changes.

To our secular age it may seem strange that people felt so strongly about theological niceties, but in the sixteenth century religion was fundamental – not so much the ware and woof of society as the very canvas onto which the threads of life's tapestry were sewn. The Reformation created a fissure that ran right through England's political centre.

Merchants smuggled Luther's books in from the continent. The bishops sought out the forbidden volumes and made bonfires of them. Preachers denounced 'Catholic superstition' from their pulpits. Episcopal officers arrested them and put them on trial for heresy. Traditionalist clergy opposed the royal supremacy. They found themselves facing treason charges. Henry never really got his head round the clash of ideologies that was threatening to change the nation and change it fundamentally. He thought only in terms of increasing and maintaining his own power. Essentially, he wanted to have his cake and eat it: preserving his reputation as an orthodox, Catholic believer while tightening the screws on the ecclesiastical establishment. He thought he could maintain a balance by allowing heretics to be burned at the stake and dissident Catholics to be hanged, drawn and quartered. And, in any case, by 1536 he had other things to worry about.

After all he had been through, the Tudor succession was still not settled. Anne fared no better in the baby stakes than her predecessor (who was currently eking out a dismal existence in damp exile on the edge of the fens). Her first pregnancy resulted in a healthy daughter, Elizabeth, but after that she suffered two miscarriages. By the beginning of 1536 the relationship of the royal couple was more than ten years old and the first fine careless rapture had departed from it. Henry had once delighted in his lover's vivacity and wit. Now he began to be irritated by her. She was forever urging him farther along the path of reform. She also complained about the attentions he paid to other women. And to add to his problems, his health had begun to fail.

The once-slim athlete who had boasted of his exploits in the tiltyard and the (real) tennis court had become a middle-aged sluggard with a rapidly increasing girth. Only an aggressively active and competitive person who has been forced to come to terms with an ailing body can understand what Henry was going through in terms of his self-esteem. But there was worse to come. About this time Henry developed an ulcer in one of his legs. The open sore did not close and exuded evil-smelling pus. His physicians had to change his bandages on a daily basis, and his increased lameness and humiliating dependence on others did nothing to improve his temper.

The sequence of catastrophes that was to unfold so disastrously that year began with three events in January. On the sixth, Catherine, the ex-queen, died of cancer. On the 24th, Henry, refusing to abandon his self-image as a macho athlete, fell heavily during a joust at Greenwich. He was unconscious for more than two hours, having gone into the kind of coma that in the sixteenth century would often have proved fatal. Six days later Anne had her second miscarriage. The child would have been a boy. From this point it is possible to recognise only the most twisted kind of logic in Henry's actions and decisions. Once again, his desires were being thwarted. His Catholic enemies were exultant at his continuing dynastic problem. His wife was incapable of giving him a healthy son and, as his tiltyard scare demonstrated, the need for an heir was becoming rapidly more urgent. Time was not on his side. Henry decided on another change of wife. Most of his subjects had not recognised his second marriage and Anne was universally unpopular. Now he could disembarrass himself of queen number two, which would go down well in the country at large, and look for a suitable replacement. He soon found her in the person of Jane Seymour, one of the Queen's ladies-in-waiting.

Cromwell, meanwhile, was maturing his most audacious attack yet on the Church. He planned to remove the monasteries from the English landscape and divert their vast wealth into the royal coffers. At one stroke, this would remove many centres of opposition to reform and enrich the King. In February, a bill to dissolve all the smaller religious houses was put before parliament.

It was well received, largely because the wealthy landowners represented there were eager to share in the forthcoming bonanza by buying ex-monastic property from the Crown. This led to a falling out between Anne and Cromwell. The Queen was all in favour of nationalising the abbeys – but only as long as the money was put to good uses, such as education. When she recognised the land grab for what it was, she spoke out forcefully. Henry, furious at her interference in politics and her constant whinging about his affair with Jane Seymour, now turned violently against the woman for love of whom he had once defied the Pope and most of his own subjects.

It was not enough simply to wriggle out of his marriage and send Anne into some place of remote exile. Henry, seized by incontrollable rage, was determined to punish her

JOHN LAMBERT WAS BURNED BY HENRY VIII'S CHURCHMEN
IN SMITHFIELD, LONDON, THE MAIN SITE FOR THE EXECUTION
OF HERETICS.

and he cared not a whit for the fate of any others who might
be caught up in her downfall. Cromwell was instructed to
fabricate charges against her. By means of torture and
paid informers, the minister concocted an outrageous
ragout of alleged crimes, including incest, adultery with
Henry's best friend, poisoning Catherine and plotting the
King's death. On 17 May five of the Queen's alleged para-
mours were executed and she shared their fate two days later,
Henry taking a ghoulish interest in the details of their punishment. The nation went wild with joy but those in the
know were not deceived. The imperial ambassador, no friend
of Anne, reported that she was 'condemned upon presumption and certain indications, without valid proof or confession' and in the Netherlands the imperial regent shared the

belief of many that Henry 'invented this device to get rid of her'.

This barbarous act galvanised public opinion. Throughout the land the late Queen's protégés and those who shared her religious views were apprehensive, while Catholic partisans were inclined to rejoice at Anne's downfall and believed that it would stop the spread of heresy. Such people did not understand Henry VIII. He went his own erratic way, influenced only by what, moment by moment, he conceived to be in his own best interests. For the moment he placed his confidence in Cromwell, who proceeded apace with the work of reform. The first dissolution Act made quite clear the official attitude towards the religious life:

> ...manifest sin, vicious, carnal and abominable living is daily used and committed amongst the little and small abbeys, priories and other religious houses of monks, canons and nuns... the governors of such religious houses and their convent spoil, destroy, consume and utterly waste as well their churches, monasteries, priories, principal houses, farms, granges, lands, tenements and hereditaments, as the ornaments of their churches and their goods and chattels to the high displeasure of Almighty God, slander of good religion and to the great infamy of the king's Highness and the realm...

This blanket condemnation was based on the reports of inspectors who had been sent out by Cromwell with the express instruction to discover or invent stories of depravity and incompetence.

WILLIAM TYNDALE

On 6 October 1536 one of Henry's subjects was burned at the stake in Vilvoorde, near Brussels. He was destined to become, through his writings, the most influential Englishman of his age.

William Tyndale imbibed radical religious ideas at Cambridge and left with an ambition: to translate the Bible into English. The Church leaders whom Tyndale approached for help, however, rejected him because they thought that putting the Bible in the hands of ordinary people would encourage them to question what the Church taught. Tyndale had to go abroad to do his work. He played a cat-and-mouse game with the forces of reaction, moving from place to place to avoid arrest.

When he had completed the translation of the New Testament, his work had to be smuggled into England, where the bishops tried hard to track down copies and make bonfires of them.

In 1536 Tyndale was betrayed into the hands of his enemies. His last words from the stake were 'Lord, open the King of England's eyes'. Within months Henry had authorised the publication of an English Bible edited by someone sheltering cautiously behind the pseudonym of 'Thomas Matthew'. Ironically, most of the text was Tyndale's.

There certainly were faults in the system but not sufficient to justify such draconian action. It was a clear case of giving a dog a bad name and hanging him. Just as the evidence against Anne Boleyn had been manufactured, so that against the monasteries was invented in order to give the confiscation some appearance of legality. The official government line was that Henry was a white knight doing battle against the dragon of Church corruption. And it had to be backed up with massive propaganda. Cromwell set in motion a coordinated programme of books, pamphlets, sermons, songs and, probably most effective of all, the first printed lampoons, the forerunner of today's political cartoons, which pointed a critical finger at incompetent priests, lazy bishops and libidinous monks. There was no shortage of ardent preachers ready to climb on the government bandwagon in order to urge their own ideas about religious and social change:

Is it so hard, is it so great a matter for you to see many abuses in the clergy, many in the laity? Abuses... in ceremonies so often defiled by superstition; in the holidays so generally abused by drunkenness and gambling; in the images and pictures and relics and pilgrimages, encouraged by the clergy to the deception of the ignorant, in the religious rites of baptism and matrimony celebrated in an unknown tongue and not in the native language of the people...

Hugh Latimer, Bishop of Worcester, the age's most celebrated radical preacher, thus declared himself to be a champion of wide-ranging reform that would change the customs and habits of the nation.

He was a controversial figure but he was far from being alone. When a visiting preacher in Folkestone 'turned a hundred men's hearts to his opinion that the Virgin Mary could do no more for us than another woman', the town bailiff was only prevented by the vicar from yanking him out of the pulpit. The Sheriff of Gloucester complained to Cromwell of 'disorderly and colourable preaching' against purgatory, pilgrimages and offerings at the shrines of saints 'to the disquiet of Christian people'. Most of the men who gave such offence to dyed-in-the-wool conservatives had been issued by Cromwell or reformist bishops with licences to preach over large areas of the country, but there were other enthusiasts who, encouraged by the changing mood of the times, climbed into the pulpit or stood in market places to rant out their own ideas.

Some opponents of change were bold enough to set up rival orators to challenge the preachers of 'novelties' but this only resulted in pulpit wars and slanging matches, which generated more heat than light and added to the growing unease and confusion throughout the country. Thomas Audley, who became Lord Chancellor in 1535, grumbled to Cranmer that 'these new preachers... have made and brought in such divisions and seditions among us as never was seen in this realm, for the devil reigneth over us now'. One had to be careful airing such views. Audley's predecessor, Thomas More, a fanatical persecutor of heretics, had forfeited his head for refusing to endorse the King's religious policy.

These arguments did not just affect the political class. Every parish in England was turned upside down by the new ideas and reactionary responses to them. The principal evil on which reformers focused was 'idolatry'. For centuries, popular superstitious nonsense had gone unchallenged in Britain.

Simple people throughout the land bowed and scraped to garishly painted statues and went off on pilgrimage to gawp at gilded reliquaries supposedly containing bits and pieces of long-dead saints; and the reformers knew that a more informed, biblical faith would never take hold until English men and women were weaned away from such absurdities.

Even more infuriating to them were the monks who ran the 'shrine business' and collected offerings from gullible pilgrims who believed that their donations were buying themselves divine favour. As one reformer recognised, 'in churches everywhere images are honoured' and 'old-rooted custom is so strong that, though thou preach never so often nor never so earnestly', some people will still 'put off their caps unto them or else bow and make curtsey to them'.

Visual stimuli always make a more immediate impact than words. And back in the sixteenth century, the majority of people, especially the less well educated, actually believed that material things could be invested with holiness. The saints, even Christ himself, could be venerated through images. Only a very thin line (if any line at all) separates veneration through material things with worship of material things, i.e. idolatry. Church leaders had always been aware of this danger. Unfortunately, they had found it easier to encourage the practice, and benefit financially from it, than to purge the Church of objects and rituals which a more rational age was now about to expose.

As Cromwell's agents toured England's abbeys and pilgrimage centres, they confiscated numerous objects of superstition and sent them to London. They included the chains with which St Peter was bound, the coals over which St Laurence was roasted, St Edmund's toe-nail clippings, St Thomas Becket's penknife and enough fragments of the true cross to make a whole new one and still leave some over. The government's preachers and pamphleteers had a field day exposing the gullibility of people whose faith was bound up in such irrational nonsense.

What the reformers failed to foresee was the widespread anger and distress their 'new broom' programme would create. What they were doing went far beyond clearing away irrelevant clutter from Church life. They were taking a sledgehammer to the very fabric of medieval Catholicism. People's lives revolved around Church rituals and the familiar pattern of the ecclesiastical calendar. They and their forefathers had scrimped and saved to decorate their churches with paintings, statues and altar furnishings. They had paid priests to say requiem masses for their dead relatives. Women had bought relics in the belief that they would see them safely through childbirth. Farmers had prayed to specific saints when their livestock fell sick. Men and women were employed on monastic estates. When the King's preachers denounced the prevailing system, listeners grew angry – either because they believed them and were furious at having been conned by the religious establishment or because they did not believe them and were indignant at having their convictions assailed by 'heretics'.

The majority of the King's subjects were probably bewildered, no longer knowing what they were expected to believe. Some, doubtless, lapsed into scepticism. But the people who hit the 'headlines' were the minority of violent radical extremists.

Like latter-day animal rights activists, convinced that the rightness of their cause absolves them from the restraints of civil or moral law, they visited their wrath on the symbols of the old faith. They tore down statues, smashed shrines and threw holy pictures out into the street. Such extremists presented the regime with a dilemma. Cromwell needed men of conviction but zealots who went too far gave the reform movement a bad name. There was always the fear of backlash from Catholic vigilantes.

There were atrocities on both sides. In the small hours of a misty November morning, Robert Packington, a member of parliament well known for his anticlerical views, was shot dead outside his house in Cheapside. He was probably the first victim in London to be murdered by a firearm.

Back at court the euphoria of Henry's life with his new, young wife (they were married within two weeks of Anne Boleyn's execution) was soon punctured. In the issue of the succession he had always had a fallback position. Henry did have a son, a seventeen-year-old illegitimate boy named Henry Fitzroy, Duke of Richmond. The lad had received a good education, and had been given several state appointments. Though the duties were carried out by others in his name, he had gained considerable experience of various aspects of government and he was being initiated into foreign diplomacy. If all else failed, the King could have and probably would have nominated Richmond as his heir. But, in July 1536, the young man died. By the annulment

HANS HOLBEIN

Henry VIII celebrated his victory over the northern rebels by commissioning a mural from his court painter, Hans Holbein. The huge painting that dominated the privy chamber at Whitehall Palace showed Henry with his parents and his new wife, Jane Seymour, arranged around a marble plinth.

A Latin inscription praised Henry for purifying the English Church, a defiant gesture to those Pilgrims of Grace who had dared to question his religious settlement. More importantly, this, now lost, portrait was the template for the full-length, belligerent portrayal of Henry that was to become the standard image of this King.

of his two marriages (his union with Anne had been declared void), Henry had bastardised both of his daughters, so there was now no-one he was prepared to allow to succeed him. It was more than ever vital that Jane should do her stuff and do it quickly. But the months slipped past and anxious court watchers waited in vain for news of a royal pregnancy.

Meanwhile Cromwell's religious policy began to bite hard. His commissioners went efficiently and officiously about the business of closing down 374 smaller monasteries. Groups of workmen turned up to inventory the contents, remove the furnishings, strip lead from roofs, melt down the bells, make bonfires of service books and surplus timber, crate up vestments and altar fittings and pack them onto carts along with anything else that might have some value.

Locals watched anxiously. They were not so much outraged by the sacrilege (one problem Cromwell's people had was stopping pilfering) or even concerned for the fate of the dispossessed religious as worried about their own livelihoods. Some of them were abbey tenants. Others had been employed in various capacities by the monks. They worried about how they would be treated by the new owners.

The removal of the religious left holes in the social fabric, just as the disappearance of conventual buildings left gaps in the landscape. Monks had served as vicars in nearby parishes. Abbots and priors had been members of the local elite. Now they had gone and the owners of adjacent lands were already vying for parts of the spoils. Added to this was the growing suspicion that Henry's acquisitiveness would not stop when he had pocketed the proceeds of the lesser monasteries. Cromwell's agents had already begun an ominous inspection of all the remaining religious houses.

Henry was affronted and surprised by the conflict he had created. Total egotist that he was, he thought that he could simply order his subjects what to believe. He instructed his bishops to draw up a statement of officially approved religion. The Church leaders argued furiously over this but, in August 1536, they did manage to cobble together Ten Articles of faith designed, it was claimed, to ensure that 'all occasion of dissent and discord... be repressed and utterly extinguished'.

The regulations which accompanied the publication of these articles suggest that Cromwell was not as convinced as his master that people would meekly accept the royal redefinition of the ancient faith. Public comment was suppressed. The preaching of sermons was totally banned until the end of September, and after this cooling-off period preachers were warned not to interpret the new regulations 'after their own fantastical appetites'. Meanwhile commissioners were sent around the country to gather clergy together and explain to them exactly what was and was not PC religion.

But any suggestion that the new approved definition of Christian faith and practice was intended to steer a middle course between conservative and radical opinion was shot to pieces by the next government initiative. Cromwell issued, in the King's name, a set of injunctions intended to transform the life of the local church. Clergy were instructed to buy a copy of the Bible in English (until very recently,

Henry had burned people for possessing copies of Tyndale's forbidden New Testament) and to teach them the basics of the faith by rote learning. They were to discourage their flocks from going on pilgrimage, venerating saints and buying relics. Several saints' days and holy days were abolished.

Reports arriving on Cromwell's desk told of growing unease in various parts of the country. There was also disturbing news from abroad. In distant Rome the Pope was vigorously trying to bring the renegade English nation back to heel. Through diplomatic channels he was urging Catholic sympathisers to resist their heretic King and trying to persuade the rulers of France and the Holy Roman Empire to join in a crusade against England. The leading English Catholic propagandist was the self-exiled Reginald Pole. In 1536, copies of Pole's book attacking Henry's policy, asserting papal authority over the English Church and implying that good Catholics should refuse obedience to their King, were circulating in scholarly circles. Henry sent agents to the continent to arrest or, failing that, to assassinate the troublemaker, but Pole evaded capture. In December, the Pope added insult to injury by making Pole a cardinal.

By October feelings in several places were reaching flashpoint. Fire first broke out in Lincolnshire. The people of this remote shire found themselves being intolerably 'prodded' by a three-pronged governmental trident. As well as commissioners come to 'educate' the local clergy and others briefed to evaluate the wealth of the remaining monasteries, a third set of agents was busy collecting the latest tax approved by parliament.

Rumours were rife about what the legislators in distant London were really about: churches were going to be closed down or, at least, despoiled of their ancient treasures, new taxes were going to be introduced, fees previously paid for baptisms, weddings and funerals would now go to the Treasury. So crazy were the actions of a king who had cast off one wife, murdered another and declared himself to be a mini-pope that it must have seemed that he was capable of anything.

The storm burst in the fenland town of Louth. The Louthians were especially proud of their church and everything connected with it. Two generations of parishioners had worked hard and raised funds to embellish the building and especially to erect a fine new spire. At the end of September the townsfolk gathered for the Michaelmas procession through the streets, with their banners and silver crosses and jewel-encrusted reliquaries. It only took someone to shout out, 'Follow the crosses! God knows if we shall ever follow them again!' for celebration to be turned into protest.

The mob hid their precious objects and gathered to confront the King's men. Within days the demonstration had spread throughout the fenland. Bells were rung to summon the people to defend their traditions. Armed men in various centres confronted the local gentry, the guardians of law and order. The mood became nasty. Blood was shed. And Henry's subjects, while protesting their loyalty, made their demands:

1. No more taxes (the universal mantra of rebels)
2. No more suppression of monasteries

3.   The surrender to the common people of Cromwell
     and the King's other 'evil advisers'.

Henry panicked. At the time of the Peasants' Revolt
(1381) Richard II had ridden out in person to confront the
rebels. In 1487 and 1497 Henry VII had led his own army
against the forces raised by disloyal subjects. In 1536 Henry
VIII scurried off to his stoutest fortress at Windsor and from
there sent urgent and sometimes contradictory messages to
his generals and lambasted them for what he considered
their incompetence.

So paranoid and suspicious was he that he ordered his
commander-in-chief, the Duke of Norfolk, to leave his sons
behind as hostages when he rode north. He knew the Duke
for a traditionalist and an enemy of Cromwell and could not
be certain that he would not make common cause with the
rebels.

Well might he feel nervous. He assumed that the
Lincolnshire rebels would follow the pattern set by earlier
malcontents; that is that they would march to London, their
numbers growing with every southward mile. Reports coming from the Home Counties indicated that householders
were ready to sustain the 'heroes' with food and drink. Only
five miles from Windsor a butcher was arrested for declaring
that his best meat would be ready for 'the good fellows of the
north'; while a nearby parish priest boldly announced from
the pulpit that the insurrectionists were 'God's people, who
did fight and defend God's quarrel'.

In fact, the Lincolnshire Rising was over almost as soon as
it had begun. Its leaders lacked charisma and strategy. The
rebels, disorganised and frightened by their own temerity,

abandoned their cause and drifted back to their homes. Henry was unable to leave well alone, however, and allow the disaffection to evaporate. He had his uncompromising response to the rebels' demands read out to them:

> How presumptuous are ye, the rude commons of one shire, and that one of the most brute and beastly of the whole realm, and of least experience, to find fault with your prince...

He demanded a vicious purge of the disaffected region. He wanted many heads to roll. His officers on the ground were more merciful, and that for a very good tactical reason. They knew that victory in the east Midlands had been a close run thing. The forces at the King's disposal were outnumbered. If the rebels had been better organised they would have forced the royal army to retreat before reinforcements, including artillery, could have reached them from the south. Nor were the King's captains fully confident in their own men, who had little taste for killing their fellow countrymen. It would have taken little for substantial numbers to defect to the enemy. More importantly, they knew that the trouble was not over. The Lincolnshire Rising was a mere curtain-raiser. Beyond the Humber a more serious revolt was brewing. If they were to march farther north to deal with that it would not be politic to leave behind them a savaged county smouldering with resentment.

Norfolk continued onwards into Yorkshire at the head of 8,000 men. He was alarmed to receive reports that before him lay a rebel host of 40,000, who had already captured the Archbishop of York and Lord Darcy, one of the region's leading peers, and taken possession of Hull, York and Pontefract. This second revolt was also better organised

Several major landowners and nobles were sympathetic to or actively involved in the movement which soon took the name the Pilgrimage of Grace. The insurgents wished to be seen, not as rebels, but as holy pilgrims, contending for the pure faith against the King's heretical advisers. Moreover, the area involved in this case was much larger.

By mid-December, a third of England, from the und-rained marshland along the Don to Hadrian's Wall, was in arms or awaiting the call to arms. The alienation of the north went deeper and was more multi-faceted than that of Lincolnshire.

The people of this remote region had always looked more to their local aristocrats, the Percies and the Nevilles, than to whatever dynasty happened to be in possession of the throne. They did not associate closely with the political process. Parliament met hundreds of miles away and MPs had to go to the expense of travelling to and finding accommodation in the capital whenever they were summoned by the King. Northerners regarded themselves as a forgotten people. Commercially as well as politically they were at a disadvantage. London merchants dominated the nation's business life and creamed off most of the profits.

There had been little penetration of radical ideas into the north. The religious debate had scarcely begun, so that few people understood anything of the fundamental issues at stake. They were simply confused by a government apparently intent on tearing apart their traditional way of life.

Norfolk was between a rock and a hard place. Since he

did not dare to confront the rebels in open battle the only alternative was negotiation. But the King was insistent that his disobedient subjects should be crushed. Under the circumstances the Duke did the only thing he could; he summoned the rebels to meet with him to explain their grievances, while assuring Henry that this was only a ruse. 'None oath or promise made for policy to serve you, mine only master and sovereign,' he wrote to the King, 'can [corrupt] me, who shall rather be torn in a million pieces than to show one point of cowardice or untruth to your majesty.'

Norfolk was terrified of Henry – and with good reason. Henry had recently lashed out ruthlessly against Anne Boleyn – Norfolk's niece. In meetings at Doncaster he sweet-talked the rebels, now led by Robert Aske, a forceful Yorkshire lawyer, into believing that the King would pay close attention to their demands and would pardon their presumption if they dispersed. This Aske and his men began to do.

Back in London, Henry was hoping that he had got away with it, that the northerners, like the men of Lincolnshire, would prove to have no real stomach for a fight and that the onset of winter would finally undermine their resolve. But he was by no means confident. The capital was, of course, buzzing with news of the trouble in the distant shires. He, therefore, responded with public demonstrations of extravagant kingliness, while privately yielding to pressure. On 22 December he staged a magnificent progress through the City. Such a sight had not been seen for many years, according to a contemporary chronicler:

The streets were hanged with arras and cloth of gold. Priests in their copes with crosses and censers stood on one side and the citizens on the other. It rejoiced every man wondrously.

Christmas at Greenwich was kept in a style more sumptuous and extravagant than it had been for a long time. But behind the scenes the King was anxiously trying to disarm criticism. He gave orders that 123 condemned monasteries should be reprieved, including – surprise, surprise – 48 in Lincolnshire and Yorkshire. He had leading radical preachers locked up and ordered Latimer to preach at St Paul's Cross (the main platform for official religious propaganda) a sermon which stressed 'unity without any special note of any man's folly'.

Messages sent to all the bishops assured them of the King's absolute orthodoxy and rejection of all heretical ideas. At the same time, Henry invited Aske to come to court, where he publicly embraced the rebel leader and 'received him into his favour and gave unto him apparel and great rewards'. He indicated that he would summon a parliament to meet, not in London, but at York, where all the pilgrims' concerns would be addressed.

Aske was completely taken in and travelled back to his own county to spread the good news of the King's gracious concern for the wellbeing of his subjects. Others were not so convinced. One of Aske's colleagues, Sir Francis Bigod, collected together bands of erstwhile pilgrims and told them that the King was hoodwinking them. He assured them that Henry had no intention of keeping his word to pardon the petitioners or to consider their demands in a specially convened parliament. On the contrary, he had ordered Norfolk to return at the head of a larger army, track down the dispersed rebels and slaughter them mercilessly.

What is interesting about Bigod is that he was a religious radical and had been one of Cromwell's agents. Now, however, he had come to realise that neither King nor minister were to be trusted. Bigod changed sides because he was furious to see his fellow countrymen being duped by a rapacious monarch. By mid-January he had relit the fires of rebellion in several places.

This action played completely into Henry's hands. Now he had every excuse to tear up any assurances he had given to Aske and let slip the dogs of royal vengeance. But he still could not afford to be cocksure. What he could, and did, do was send Norfolk back across the Trent with ambiguous instructions so that, if the situation disintegrated further, he could blame his representative for being too harsh or too lenient. The Duke was to harry the north mercilessly but, if any arrests threatened to provoke a backlash, he was to 'look through his fingers at their offences and free them… till the king's majesty's arrival in these parts'.

Norfolk spent the next few weeks ferreting out offenders, arraigning them before courts martial, carrying out executions and writing frequent letters to the King to draw attention to his zeal.

He boasted of his arbitrary selection of victims and their hasty despatch. If he had proceeded through the usual courts, he said, the judges would have had to listen to the defendants' excuses – 'I joined the rebellion out of fear of my life or out of fear of the loss of all my goods or out of regard for the safety of my family'. Martial law was for more efficient, expeditious – and ruthless.

The last major incident of the Pilgrimage of Grace was the pilgrims' attempt to seize Carlisle. This had more to do with local grievances against northern landlords than issues of religious principle. The ill-armed rebels were routed by local gentry. They cut down hundreds of men trying to escape across the fields and took over 300 prisoners. Norfolk knew well that this latest demonstration was not aimed at the king but it provided him with an opportunity to give Henry bloody proof of his loyalty. Seventy-four culprits – all poor men, farm labourers and artisans – were hanged in their own villages, 'in trees in their gardens', to drive home that royal vengeance had long arms.

There were so many executions that not enough chains could be found with which to suspend the bodies. Rope had to be substituted. A historian of the northern rebellion commented, 'This is the final indictment of Henry's government, that his greatest nobleman hanged men whom he knew to be guilty only of having turned against intolerable oppression.' The plan was that the corpses would remain strung up for months, their stinking decomposition providing a lingering warning to all potential malcontents.

The King claimed the suppression of the rebels as a great personal victory. Of course he had been lucky to get away with it but, certainly, no-one from that time forward would seriously contemplate opposing England's increasingly paranoid monarch.

1536 was the year the King went mad, the year that demonstrated that no-one was safe, not queen or courtier, minister or general, monk or priest, peer or peasant. One of the ways Henry chose to celebrate was by having a new, full-length portrait painted by his court painter, Hans

Holbein. It depicted the King, sumptuously dressed, hands on hips and glaring defiantly from the canvas. It is the image of him with which, almost 500 years later, we are all familiar.

What Happened Before...

1648 ROTTENEST YEAR

...And What Came After

1648

CIVIL WAR IS the worst disaster that can befall a nation. There is not a city, not a town, not a village, not a street, not a farmstead, not a home, not a family that remains untouched. At the beginning of 1648, men, women and children throughout the British Isles were trying to come to terms with six years of war that had forced every one of them to take sides for king or parliament. They were mourning their dead. There had been 645 separate military confrontations, and when deaths from war-related disease are added to battlefield casualties the number comes out at around a quarter of a million dead. That means that, viewed as a percentage of the population, more British people died in this conflict than in the First World War. The survivors were struggling to bring neglected fields back under cultivation and to restock decimated herds and flocks. Farms had been rendered unworkable by the depredations of the armies that marched to and fro, demanding to be fed. People were contemplating the ruins of a fractured society. England, Wales and Ireland were, in effect, under military rule. The war had sundered neighbour from neighbour, master from apprentice, father from son, brother from brother. But, now, at last, a start could be made on getting back to some semblance of normality. For the war was over.

The royalist forces had been defeated eighteen months previously. The initiative had passed from officers in the field to peacemakers around the negotiating table. King Charles I was in custody on the Isle of Wight and was in discussions with his enemies. There was a real possibility that the armies that had devastated large tracts of the country would be disbanded and the soldiers sent home. It seemed that a constitutional settlement of some sort could be hammered out allowing parliamentarians and royalists to live together for the wellbeing of the nation. In short, for the first time in years people allowed themselves to hope. What made 1648 such a cruel year was that that hope was shattered.

The leaders of parliament and the parliamentary army believed that they had successfully isolated Charles from his supporters. He would not be able to lead his troops. An attempt to escape from Carisbrooke the previous year had been a laughable failure: the fastidious King had been unwilling to squeeze himself through a narrow window. His captors thought that they had successfully blocked his contacts with royalist activists. They had Charles where they wanted him and could force him to reach an agreement limiting his powers and obliging him to rule in partnership with the representatives of the people. They were mistaken. Charles had no intention of being anything less than an absolute monarch. He actually spent much of his time in captivity designing a sumptuous new residence for himself to replace the existing

Whitehall Palace. To ensure his return to power he was intent on sowing divisions among his enemies. One party he had to deal with was the representatives of the Scottish parliament, for Scotland was, at that time, a separate kingdom. In December 1647 he made a secret deal with the Scots. It was called the Engagement. In return for making certain concessions over religion, they pledged themselves to come to his aid with an army of 40,000. The Engagement was sealed in lead and buried in the grounds of the castle while the Scottish representatives returned home to organise an invasion.

When news of these dealings leaked out, in April 1648, all hell broke loose. Parliament leaders felt utterly betrayed, while their opponents were encouraged to renew the conflict. In Wales, royalists raised the standard of revolt. In various parts of England men loyal to the Stuart royal family, or who simply hated the new rulers in Westminster, sharpened their swords and took their armour out of storage. The carnage was about to begin all over again. 1648 became a depressing year of renewed bloodshed, political chaos and unrelieved fear. For many war-weary British people it seemed that they were trapped in a dark, locked room to which no-one had a key.

'Kings – can't live with 'em; can't live without 'em.' That just about sums up the reasons for the 'English Civil War' (which was actually at least two wars and, since it spread to every part of the British Isles, was certainly not just 'English'). Historians love to write about 'causes', and the differences between king and parliament involved several issues of taxation, religion and civil liberties. But what the bloody carnage actually came down to was a conflict of ideas about sovereignty. Charles, who came to the throne in 1625, was by no means an intellectual, but when he developed a conviction about something, he clung to it dogmatically. He had been brought up by his father, James I (1603-1625), to believe in what was, to him, a shiningly obvious conviction about what it meant to be a king. James Stuart had been King of Scotland before inheriting the English crown on the death of Elizabeth I. Political traditions in the two countries were very different. North of the border the King ruled from his court by playing off against each other factions of nobles and senior clergy. In England the balance of power was much more subtle: monarch, Privy Council, House of Lords and House of Commons were like intermeshed cogs in a delicate machine which, on the whole, worked smoothly, but which could seize up if any one part got out of synch. James totally failed to understand the difference. He mistakenly believed that he had escaped the constraints placed upon him in his northern kingdom and could now, in effect, do whatever he liked. For example, when during his journey from Edinburgh to London in 1603, a cutpurse was arrested in the crowd at Newark, James ordered his summary execution and genuinely found it difficult to understand that, in England, everyone from the king downwards was subject to the law.

James was an intense thinker: very good on theory but hopelessly inept at understanding how and when theories can be put into practice – and how and when they can't. Henry IV, the extremely pragmatic King of France (1589-1610), rightly dismissed his brother monarch as 'the wisest fool in Christendom'. James solemnly laid out his principles of kingship in books – *Basilicon Doron* ('Royal Gift') and *The Trew Law of Free Monarchies* – designed as working manuals for his successor. The fixed point around which James' thinking revolved was that 'kings are God's lieutenants upon earth and sit upon God's throne' exercising 'a manner of resemblance of God's power on earth'. He stated his theory explicitly to parliament:

> God hath power to create or destroy, make or unmake at his pleasure, to give life or send death, to judge all and to be judged or accountable to none…and the like power have kings: they make and unmake their subjects: they have power of raising and casting down: of life and death: judges over all their subjects and in all causes and yet accountable to none but God only.

Elizabeth I, while never allowing parliament to usurp royal powers, had always handled the Lords and Commons with tact. 'Tact' was not a word that James understood or thought it necessary to employ in dealing with his people. He tended to lecture parliament. When he tried to limit their freedom of speech, telling them what they were and were not permitted to discuss, relations became strained. He was, however, always careful not to push them too far.

Charles, by contrast, being less intelligent, saw no need to avoid confrontation. He had swallowed his father's 'divine right of kings' theory hook, line and sinker and, when he succeeded James in 1625 he asserted his authority unequivocally. But parliament's leaders had, by now, defined their position more clearly. 'The people are, under God, the original of all just power' and 'whatsoever is enacted and declared for law by the Commons in parliament assembled has the force of law'. (The words are from a declaration of 1649 but are an accurate statement of the principle for which the parliamentarians went to war.) So sovereignty is either top down or bottom up, depending on how you look at it. It cannot be both. Compromise between irreconcilable principles is impossible. Unless the royal irresistible force or the parliamentarian immovable object gave way there was going to be an almighty bang.

No-one wanted the explosion and, despite several clashes between Charles and the representatives of the voting class (principally major landowners and wealthy merchants), it did not happen for seventeen years. This was largely because, for eleven of those years (1629-1640) the King ruled without parliament. Having found himself at odds with them over several issues, he simply accused the members of the Commons of sedition and dismissed them. Now lacking all restraint, he pursued more extreme policies and financed his despotism from the levying of indirect taxes which he claimed was his prerogative. He also approved the moving of Anglican worship in a more ritualistic direction, which those of his subjects who were dubbed 'Puritans' regarded as merely Roman Catholicism in disguise (Charles' wife, Henrietta Maria, was a Catholic.)

But the King could not put off the confrontation indefinitely because he could not collect ordinary taxation without parliamentary consent. Sooner or later, he would need money and when the agitators against his 'tyranny' met again in the Commons chamber, they would demand redress of certain specified grievances. In the event, Charles dug his own grave by precipitate – and costly – action against his Scottish subjects. He decided that they should worship in the same way as his people south of the border. In other words, they should become Anglicans. But many of them were Presbyterians. Their churches were governed by ministers and each congregation was autonomous. There was no way they were going to accept rule by bishops and, in 1638, they united in the National Covenant to oppose all the innovations being imposed upon them. The King decided to meet this 'heretical rebellion' with force. Armies cost money and it was to continue his war against the Covenanters, as they were called, that Charles was obliged to summon parliament in 1640. His military predicament was made worse when rebellion broke out in Ireland. Parliament now had the King over a barrel and they wrung several concessions from him before he decided that enough was enough. In August 1642, he raised the royal standard at Nottingham and summoned loyal subjects to come to his aid against his disobedient parliament. For the first time in 157 years, Englishmen took the field against Englishmen.

The war that followed did not just result in defeat for the royalists; it further complicated the political situation. By 1648, the conflict was not just between king and parliament. The Scottish Covenanters had their own agenda: they now wanted to impose their form of church government south of the border and they had many Presbyterian supporters in the Commons. Parliament, therefore, suffered from internal divisions and was also at odds with its own soldiers. But there was now a new political force in the land. The highly efficient New Model Army that parliament, called into being to fight the royalists, showed no sign of agreeing to be disbanded until its own specific demands were met. Men who had risked their lives and seen their comrades fall in battle were suspicious that MPs would do a deal over their heads. But there was no agreed 'army policy'. Troubled times had thrown up several barrack room lawyers with their own ideas about the country's political future. The legislators at Westminster were now worried that they had created a monster bent on establishing a military dictatorship. As if that were not bad enough, the collapse of the constitution had thrown up a host of religious and political sects – sects with such disturbing names as Levellers, Diggers, Ranters and Fifth Monarchy Men. Britain was in a state of chaos with wild-eyed 'prophets' springing up everywhere, fanatical preachers claiming a hotline to god. It seemed, as one commentator observed, that the world had been turned upside down. So, although fighting had come to an end with the surrender of the last royalist army in June 1646, the road to a negotiated settlement was certain to be long and strewn with obstacles. All the interested parties were involved in talks that were rendered fruitless by their irreconcilable ambitions. Furthermore, in a country lacking direction from the centre, regional law and order had broken down and there were frequent outbreaks of local mob violence.

The renewal of the nation's agonies began at Christmas 1647. Or, perhaps it would be more accurate to call it non-Christmas 1647. Parliament was now controlled by the 'Puritans' (so-called because of their desire to purify personal and corporate religion of all superstitious and worldly distractions from the simple truth of the Gospel, as they understood it). Among the casualties of their stern code were 'unnecessary and frivolous' traditional feasts and holidays. Included in the celebrations they abolished was Christmas. This, of course, did not go down well with the general public and the end of December brought riots in various places. Troops had to be despatched to protect Puritan clergy proclaiming the government's party line from their pulpits. At Canterbury, labourers refused to turn up for work on 25 December and most trades-men declined to open their shops. The few who did comply were confronted by a threatening mob who threw their goods out onto the street. The ringleaders were arrested but broke out of jail, doubtless aided by sympathisers who had access to the keys. Later in the day, soldiers joined with townsmen for a football match that rushed through the streets and quickly turned into a nasty riot. City fathers were chased to their own front doors and a minister was pelted with mud. From Canterbury the unrest rapidly spread in widening circles. Prominent men of the county joined in what soon became a royalist rising. 'For God and the King!' went up the cry. Surprisingly, there are no reports of any fatalities, but this was only the first of a series of disturbances to break out in a country that was ungoverned and ungovernable.

But more important events were taking place elsewhere that Christmastide. While his enemies were hopelessly divid-ed and while parliamentary and army leaders were earnestly looking for some constitutional formula which would allow the King to keep his crown while being stripped of some of his powers, Charles was still scheming. His confinement at Carisbrooke was far from onerous. He was free to wander about the island under guard and he even had his carriage brought across from the mainland. He had several attendants and many of the islanders were sympathetic. He thought of himself as holding court on the Isle of Wight. When he re-ceived delegations from parliament, the army or the Scots, he could convince himself that they had come as dutiful sub-jects to pay their humble respects. He was determined to play off the opposition parties against each other by promising to give each group what it wanted in return for his restoration.

Everyone involved in these negotiations was frustrated by his slipperiness. But they were caught between a rock and a hard place; if they found it infuriating to deal with him, they certainly could not deal without him.

In the end, Charles decided that the Covenanters were his best option. In the Engagement which he signed on 26 December, Charles promised to make Presbyterianism the state religion for a trial period of three years. This complete reversal of the situation that had started the war in the first place was a cynical piece of realpolitik. The King, who was, after all, head of the Church of England, calculated that once the Covenanters had reopened hostilities, everyone discontented with parliament and the New Model Army would flock to his banner. When his allies had given him his victory he would be able to discard them and renege on his promise.

Fresh plans were made to get Charles away from the island. At the end of December everything was ready for him to be smuggled aboard a fishing boat, but the scheme was dashed by a sudden change of wind direction. Only when another bungled escape attempt in February was discovered did the authorities become alarmed. But more alarming still was the news of military preparations which arrived from Edinburgh. The threat of war threw the cat among the pigeons, as Charles had hoped it would. His strategy (if such it could be called) was that his alliance with the Scots would re-energise his supporters south of the border and that this would result either in the defeat of his enemies or that it would panic the parliamentary majority into proposing fresh concessions in order to avoid further death and destruction. His assessment of the situation was correct – as far as the politicians in Westminster were concerned. What he completely underestimated was the response of the army leaders. They had been pushed beyond the point of endurance. Charles Stuart had finally exposed himself as 'that man of blood', whose word could never be trusted and who proposed to unleash fresh horrors on a land that had already suffered more than enough. These were the men who had seen their own sons and brothers, friends and servants fall in battle in the war against tyranny. They were resolved that their comrades should not have suffered in vain. In April, the army council rejected finally any idea of negotiation. The King must be 'brought to account for the blood he had shed and the mischief he had done'.

Ardent royalists, of course, were heartened by the latest turn of events. They were further encouraged by the escape of James, Duke of York, the fourteen-year-old son of Charles, the only member of the royal family not to have already fled to France. He was being 'honourably detained' at St James's Palace. One day in April a game

All but one of London's playhouses were pulled down. Actors caught defying the law were ordered to be whipped and anyone attending a performance faced a hefty fine.

of hide-and-seek was devised for his entertainment. While he was out of sight of his minders, supporters spirited him away to join his mother and elder brother on the continent. With the Stuart dynasty secure, there was some hope for a return to monarchical government, whatever happened to Charles. For dyed-in-the-wool traditionalists this was the only solution to the nation's problems. They continued to denounce the nation's current parliament in sermons, pamphlets and popular ballads. One broadsheet prematurely published a hopeful obituary:

> *Here lies the ruins (who can but lament?)*
> *Of England's mad and bloody parliament.*
> *Here lies rebellion, murder, sacrilege,*
> *Here are the Achans* stole the golden wedge.*
> *Here lie the grand impostors of our nation,*
> *Who surfeited with too much revelation.*
> *Here lies ambition, envy, pride and lust,*
> *All huddled up in this rebellious dust.*

The royalists had a great deal of support, not because people longed for the return of an autocrat, but because they blamed all the nation's current ills on the government. When they had to pay crippling taxes to sustain the war effort, ordinary folk decided they were worse off than they had been under Stuart autocracy. Poor harvests added to the dislocations of war to drive up prices. The cost of living in the late 1640s rose by 45 per cent.

What made hardship more difficult to bear was that England, Scotland, Wales and the Irish Pale were governed by the Puritans. They were, to all intents and purposes, theocracies in which the legislators believed it their duty to uphold public morals as well as keep the peace and punish crime. There was nothing unusual about that. Members of parliament, no less than the King, believed themselves to have a

---

* According to the Old Testament book of Joshua, Achan stole a golden bar during the sacking of Jericho, despite the fact that the victors had been ordered to destroy everything. As a result, God deserted the Israelites, who were defeated in their next battle. The moral would have been obvious to seventeenth-century readers.

responsibility to God. At a local level magistrates worked closely with religious ministers to ensure that townspeople and villagers lived lives that were both peaceable and virtuous. And they were backed by that instrument of tyranny that not even Charles had had at his disposal – a standing army. But piety and politics are uneasy bedfellows. Ordinary folk whose religion was not particularly intense resented the 'rule of the saints', those they branded as 'Puritans'. This had actually become a catch-all term of contempt.

> If any gentleman in his country maintained the good laws of the land or stood up for any public interest in his country, for good order of government, he was a Puritan... all that crossed the interest of the needy courtiers, the proud encroaching priests... the lewd nobility and gentry, whoever was zealous for God's glory or worship, could not endure blasphemous oaths, ribald conversation, profane scoffs, Sabbath breach, derision of the word of God and the like; whoever could endure... anything that was good, all these were Puritans, and if Puritans then enemies to the king and his government, seditious factious hypocrites, ambitious disturbers of the public peace and finally the pests of the kingdom, enemies of God and good men...

That description by Lucy Hutchinson, widow of one of the parliamentary generals, gives a pretty fair impression of the deep hatreds and suspicions that were sapping the strength and vitality from British society.

Of course, sometimes the 'godly' deserved the taunt of hypocrisy. In October 1648, a broadsheet exposed Myles Corbet, one of the leading Puritan parliamentarians. He was caught with a prostitute and set upon by a couple of enraged gentlemen. When this came to the attention of the other members of the Commons, they closed ranks behind their colleague and 'voted it a high breach of privilege for any member to be robbed of his minion, or in any way else to be affronted, assaulted or diverted from his pleasure'. Corbet's attackers were arrested. Such anecdotes made it virtually impossible for the government to win respect and cooperation for their task of creating a godly commonwealth.

Those who were against the government took frequent opportunities to demonstrate their displeasure. The local authorities had to be constantly on their guard, responding to and, where possible, anticipating mob violence. Any gathering of a large number of people had to be very carefully policed. For this reason the theatres had been closed in 1647. It was all too easy for playwrights and popular actors to use the stage as a 'pulpit' from which to denounce or lampoon their Puritan masters. They were the media celebrities of their day. Just as modern press columnists and TV 'investigators' deliberately play to the gallery by attacking those in power, so those who controlled the playhouses were adept at undermining authority figures. As soon as the ban was lifted in January 1648, crowds flocked to the reopened theatres. But not for long. On 11 February, the edict was reissued. This time it was followed by more draconian action. All but one of the London playhouses were pulled down. Actors caught defying the law were ordered to be whipped and anyone attending a performance faced a swingeing fine. The conflict between religious zealots and the theatrical 'lovies' had been going on ever since Shakespeare had created the pompous Malvolio and Ben Jonson had poked fun at the humbuggery of Zeal-of-the-Land

Busy. It was not going to stop now. The apparent triumph of the guardians of public order and morality only drove the actors underground and ensured that they and their patrons allied themselves with the royalists. Clandestine performances in the mansions of the nobility took on the nature of political defiance. Such gatherings frequently ended with wine being passed round so that the company could drink the toast 'The King shall have his own again'.

From the spring, the mood throughout much of the country was ugly. Expressions of public belligerence became more frequent. But it was the anniversary of the King's accession (27 March) that, like the first in a line of tumbling dominoes, properly started the collapse of public order. It was celebrated enthusiastically and defiantly in several places. In London, bonfires illuminated the streets. The city became victim to the seventeenth-century equivalent of lager louts who stopped carriages and forced their occupants to drink the King's health.

This was very alarming for the city fathers and their friends at Westminster. Government vigilance was stepped up. Apprentices, particularly, had to be watched, for (like their modern student counterparts) they not infrequently formed the core of illicit demonstrations. In April, the Lord Mayor sent troops to disperse a crowd in Moorfields who were watching a game of tip-cat, and the situation rapidly got out of hand. Soon a mob of 3-4,000 led by stone-throwing apprentices were rampaging through the City. Their defiantly chanted mantra was 'For King Charles!' Rioting went on all night and the protestors were, actually, for a time, in command of the capital. It took a considerable detachment of the New Model Army to restore order.

Two weeks later it was the turn of Norwich to be up in arms. There, a royalist throng obtained control of the arsenal. Their attempt to arm themselves and cause mayhem was only frustrated when the magazine was accidentally set on fire. More than a hundred people perished in the resulting explosion.

Seven days later, on May Day, a crowd of revellers at Bury St Edmunds turned nasty when a troop of parliamentary horses rode past. Rabble-rousers shrieking, 'For God and King Charles!' led a charge of stone-throwers against the soldiers and this escalated into a riot as hundreds of men and women went wild, seeking out aldermen, their families and any neighbours believed to be sympathetic to the government.

Before the month was out there was fresh trouble south of the river. When the trial of the Christmas offenders at Canterbury took place, the jury declined to bring in a guilty verdict. The news was received with mixed emotions. Alongside general rejoicing there ran fear that government and army would go ahead regardless with their punishment of the accused. False rumours flew, fanning the flames of suspicion. Within days agitators had drawn up a petition demanding that parliament come to terms with the King, that the army be disbanded, and that the people should not be vexed with arbitrary taxes. Copies were despatched all over the county and attracted thousands of signatures. What was more alarming was the clause attached to it which threatened armed uprising if the people's demands were not met. In preparation for carrying out this threat a meeting was arranged for the end of the month at Blackheath, a traditional convergence point for rebels. Bands of activists seized strategic points

in the county. When news reached part of the naval fleet
lying in the Thames estuary, the crews mutinied. For the
government, the situation seemed to be spiralling out of
control.

On the other side of the river, the leading men of Essex
also prepared a petition asking parliament to make fresh concessions. They urged that this was the only way to remove
'all such misapprehensions and fears which are yet the un-
happy obstacles of the peace and quiet of our kingdom'. In
the capital itself the Mayor and corporation embraced the
passion for petitioning. They asked for Charles to be brought
back to Westminster, 'in honour, freedom and safety' for a
new round of negotiation. The anxious burgesses were no
different from their counterparts throughout the country,
who were desperate for a settlement – any settlement. Soon
there was scarcely a shire in the land which had not taken its
cue from the Home Counties and produced similar petitions.
Suddenly, the parliamentarians sensed themselves being surrounded, manoeuvred, their authority undermined. Much to
their chagrin, they realised that they were still dependent on
the army.

The army did not fail them. It was the only national body
that had strong leadership, discipline, political vision and
the means to enforce its will. It was certainly not immune to
division but its council derived unity from its obedience to
a higher power. They met frequently for earnest 'wrestling
in prayer' to discern God's will. Ironically, the justification they claimed was derived from their position as agents
of the Almighty; it was another version of divine right.
General Tom Fairfax took possession of Blackheath at the
end of May and prevented the royalist rebels from muster-

ing there. The hard core of the royalists, led by the Earl of Norwich, retreated to Maidstone. Fairfax pursued them. After a brief engagement, Norwich's host, rapidly dwindling, crossed the Thames in order to link up with supporters in Essex. On 12 June he took possession of Colchester. There he successfully repulsed an enemy attack. Fairfax decided not to risk further casualties by storming the impressive walls of the well-fortified town. He simply settled down to a long siege. The royalist defenders pinned their hopes on the Scots who had by now crossed the border. Norwich was sure that, as the invaders moved southwards, gathering support along their march, parliament would need all its forces to face them and would be obliged to raise the siege. It was a seriously flawed calculation.

The irony, the tragic irony, was that there was no need for the royalists to resort to force. In the spring and early summer the leaders of parliament and the army were very much on the back foot. Back in January, parliament had resolved to have nothing more to do with the devious King but Charles' alliance with the Scots had forced them to think again. At this stage no-one wanted war and no-one, except for some of the army hotheads, had any idea of establishing non-monarchical government. Some of the parliament men toyed with the idea of deposing Charles in favour of his eldest son but that was the most radical proposal on the table. Parliament, Scots, royalist activists, everyone was looking for an honourable compromise – everyone, that is, except the king.

No-one had ever told Charles that politics is the art of the possible, and he would not have believed them if they had. He was contending for an inviolable and holy principle – his right, under God, to rule as he saw fit. Even some of the army leaders, despite their denunciation of the 'man of blood', were looking for some kind of peaceful solution.

In April, an up-and-coming figure among the parliamentarians made a secret visit to the King. His name was Oliver Cromwell, MP and charismatic general, and he was hoping to persuade Charles to call off the Scottish invasion. He made no impression on the stubborn King and this may well have been the moment that sealed Charles' fate. Cromwell had constantly urged moderation in his Commons speeches and had now risked his reputation among the army by his pilgrimage to Carisbrooke. He came away saddened but hardened, convinced that God had rejected this faithless monarch and that nothing could now save him from divine judgement.

While Fairfax was involved with the military situation in the south-east, he despatched other generals to the trouble spots farther afield. At the end of May, Cromwell hurried to south Wales where a royalist rising was centred on Pembroke. He quickly dealt with the resistance in Chepstow and Tenby and captured Pembroke Castle on 11 June. Meanwhile, another officer, Major-General John Lambert, rode northwards to face the invading Scots. His advance was slowed down at Pontefract where royalists had command of the garrison. Although the Scottish commander, the Duke of Hamilton, only had 9,000 men under his command, instead of the promised 40,000, Lambert, with only 3,000 troops, could not engage him. He could only shadow the invaders and wait for reinforcements.

As soon as Cromwell had received the Welsh surrender,

THE LOCAL AUTHORITIES HAD TO BE CONSTANTLY ON THEIR GUARD,
TO ANTICIPATE AND RESPOND TO MOB VIOLENCE.

he marched his men across England to join Lambert. Even by the time the men from Wales had arrived the parliamentary contingent was still outnumbered. But the Scots now faced Oliver Cromwell and he was always worth several thousand men. After linking with Lambert at Knaresborough, he force-marched his army across the Pennines. This proved to be one of several occasions on which Cromwell's charismatic leadership and the discipline of the New Model Army really paid off. The summer of 1648 was cold, wet and beset by frequent gales. Cannon and baggage trains became bogged down. Troops easily succumbed to fevers. Their saturated clothes fell to pieces. Cromwell actually had to slow the progress of his army because his men had run out of socks and boots.

It was 17 August before he and Lambert caught up with the enemy. The Scots were also affected by the weather and the parliamentary army caught them unprepared at Preston. After a bitter four-hour engagement, Cromwell drove the royalists from the field. He divided his prisoners of war into two categories: the Scottish conscripts were allowed to make their way home, but men who had volunteered to fight for the King were shipped off to the American colonies.

This left Colchester as the only royalist stronghold still offering resistance. The defenders were in a desperate situation. When every last horse, dog and cat had been eaten, the starving citizens begged Norwich to surrender, but he refused until 27 August, by which time everyone within the walls was in dire straits. Weeks of heavy bombardment had rendered parts of the city uninhabitable, as a contemporary recorded:

> How sad a spectacle it is to see goodly buildings, well furnished houses and whole streets to be nothing but ruinous heaps of ashes and both poor and rich brought almost to the same woeful state… rich men, late of good quality, now equal to the meanest, toiling and sweating in carrying some mean bed or other away, or some inconsiderable household stuffs out of the burning, all of them with wailing and weeping, ghastly countenances and meagre, thin faces, shifting and flying in distraction of mind they scarce know whither…

For the royalist leaders who had shown such fanatical stubbornness there could be no mercy. They were immediately despatched by firing squad. One of them, Sir Charles Lucas, standing before his executioners, claimed, 'I have died in a good cause' and, years later, an inscription was added to his tomb which claimed that he had been 'in cold blood barbarously murdered'. But if there were any heroic martyrs in Colchester they were to be found among the ranks of those who lived on, obliged to struggle to rebuild their ruined businesses, homes and lives.

Colchester saw the worst horrors of the war but other locales were not far behind in their suffering. Several of the northern royalists were found lying in the muddy fields, too weary to flee any farther. In Cornwall cornered King's men dashed themselves into the sea rather than surrender.

Now the military struggle really *was* over. But its causes remained unresolved. The future was still unclear. The three-way struggle between king, parliament and army continued. Parliament persisted in believing that it could maintain its superiority by forcing the King to yield to them some of his powers.

For his part, the King was unrepentant. He still entertained hopes of escape to France. He still thought he could cynically string his enemies along with promises of reform he had no intention of honouring. Meanwhile, parliamentary agents in France reported on the activities of Queen Henrietta Maria and other exiles who were planning a fresh offensive involving foreign invasion from a base in Ireland. The army was more than ever resolved upon a drastic resolution of the nation's ills.

The initiative lay with the generals. In November they presented a 'remonstrance' to parliament, demanding that an end be made of pointless negotiation and that the King and others responsible for the wars 'be speedily brought to justice for the treason, blood and mischief' inflictedupon the country. Caught between two intransigent participants, parliament succumbed to a paralysis of will. Its members were frightened to discuss the remonstrance and watched, petrified, while army units were concentrated in and around the capital. When MPs arrived at Westminster on the morning of 6 December it was to find the palace ringed with troops and Colonel Thomas Pride standing at the entrance with a list in his hand. On it were the names of members known to be opposed to the army's position. These men, as they approached, were arrested or turned away. Others, hearing what was afoot, absented themselves. The result of 'Pride's Purge' was to restrict membership of the Commons to about 200 from its existing membership of 470. It was, to all intents and purposes, a military coup, although the pretence of representative government was maintained.

Even at this eleventh hour, the army leaders held back from pressing their action to its logical conclusion. The bloody end to which events were pushing them was unique in English history and terrible to contemplate. It might also prove to be politically inept. There were many in the parliament house and even among the upper ranks of the army who pointed out that to bring the King to trial, to find him guilty, as they inevitably would, and to punish him accordingly, far from ending the wars, would provoke a horrified backlash, uniting thousands at home and abroad against whatever constitution England's new masters might put in place. While England experienced its second non-Christmas, one final approach was made to Charles. It received the usual rebuff. And still the army council agonised and squirmed. They even called upon a celebrated proph-

THE DEATH OF CHARLES I

Charles I was not the first English king to be killed by his own subjects. Edward II (1327), Richard II (1400) and Henry VI (1471) all died violently at the hands of powerful factions who objected to their policies. What makes Charles' fate unique is that it was public. He was not removed by a clique of discontented nobles but by a parliament and army anxious to demonstrate that their action was within the law. Whether it was or not has been debated ever since.

At two o'clock on 30 January 1649, an afternoon of hard frost, King Charles I was escorted through the long banqueting hall of Whitehall Palace. He stepped through the embrasure, where a window had been removed, and onto the specially constructed scaffold outside. An enormous crowd watched in awed silence. Few can have heard the prepared speech the King made in justification of his actions. Afterwards Charles spent a moment in prayer. Then he lay down with his neck on the block. One observer who saw the axe fall remembered years later hearing 'such a groan as I never heard before and I desire I may never hear again'. Well might the people sigh; it was as though a door had been slammed and bolted on the nation's past. No-one could imagine what its future might hold.

etess, Elizabeth Poole, to advise them in the name of God. She assured them that the army had been chosen as the saviours of the nation. They should bring the King to trial – but only so that he might confront his conscience. On no account should they lay violent hands on the Lord's anointed. Few could believe that they would actually do so. Everyone in the political nation waited tensely on every scrap of news from the capital.

But before the new year was one month old, King Charles I had been publicly tried and beheaded.

What Happened Before...

1720 ROTTENEST YEAR

... And What Came After

1720

'WHO WANTS TO be a millionaire?' Before you reply 'I do', you might like to reflect how and when the word 'millionaire' entered the English language. It made its appearance in 1720, a year that should have taught the British people some long-lasting lessons about the pursuit of 'easy money'. A minority of incompetent and dishonest men brought misery to the majority and shame to the nation. Businesses went bankrupt. Workers were laid off. Families were driven into poverty. Desperate victims committed suicide. The events of this awful year made a deep impact on the whole of society. 1720 was the year the South Sea Bubble burst.

And it wasn't as if this celebrated crisis hit us out of a clear blue sky. A recent financial scandal in France had caused havoc and should have set warning bells ringing. It was the work of John Law, a Scottish fugitive from justice who had fled to the continent after killing a rival in a duel. In 1715, after some years as a professional gambler, he arrived in Paris, where he ingratiated himself with the Duc d'Orléans, the regent during the minority of Louis XV. Law's mind bristled with sure-fire financial schemes and he managed to con the government into allowing him to set up the *Compagnie des Indes*, otherwise known as the Mississippi Scheme. This began as a company enjoying monopoly trading rights to the vast Louisiana region of North America but rapidly expanded until it embraced the totality of France's international commerce outside Europe. Not satisfied with this, Law, at the beginning of 1720, assumed responsibility for the greater part of the French National Debt. His company thus became virtually the sole creditor of the French state. Law was a remarkable phenomenon, as plausible as he was genuinely talented. His enterprise took the European world by storm. Investors from all the leading countries rushed to buy shares in his company. Within months the value of those shares rose from 500 livres to 18,000 livres. Fortunes were made literally overnight and the word 'millionaire' was coined to describe the leading beneficiaries. As the Duchesse d'Orléans commented, 'Everybody speaks in millions. I don't understand it all but I see clearly that the god Mammon reigns as absolute monarch in Paris.' Soon Mississippi fever was at its height. Unfortunately, most opportunist investors were as ignorant as the Duchesse d'Orléans about how financial markets work – and, more importantly, what stops them working.

In Paris the market fell more rapidly than it had risen. Investors began to take their profits, cashing in their paper

> In the Commons, Robert Walpole accused the South Sea Company of propagating lies and fantasies, of encouraging the British people to indulge in golden dreams of limitless prosperity.

money and shares for specie. Law and his co-directors tried various measures to stop the leaching of gold but by May the company was forced to refuse payments. Panic and street riots ensued. Law, the most powerful and, possibly, the richest man in France, was driven from office and from the country. He resumed the life of a peripatetic gambler and died, in Venice, nine years later – broke.

The three decades before investment fever hit Britain had been disturbing and expensive. In 1685 the last Stuart King, James II, had been expelled in favour of his daughter, Mary, and her Dutch husband, William of Orange. The Anglo-Dutch alliance had involved Britain in wars with France and its expansionist King, Louis XIV. These had continued intermittently until 1713. The following year the reigning monarch, Queen Anne, died without heir. The quest for a suitable replacement (and 'suitable' meant firmly Protestant) brought to the throne a German prince, George Frederick of Hanover, who spoke no English and, accordingly, relied more heavily than any of his predecessors on parliament. But the exiled Stuarts had not given up their hope of regaining the crown. James II's son landed in Scotland in 1715 and headed a rebellion. It was fairly easily suppressed, but the Jacobites (supporters of James and, later, his son) continued to be a worry for their influence among Britain's enemies abroad. In 1718 the government also managed to get Britain embroiled in a brief war with Spain, this time in alliance with the old enemy, France. All these conflicts cost money.

In the earlier 'bad old days' when kings had ruled with, sometimes, little more than a nod and a wink to parliament, they obtained their income from Crown estates, direct and indirect taxation and from borrowing on the national and international money markets. For some monarchs taxation was the least attractive of these sources because it involved seeking parliamentary sanction. Lords and Commons could and did use the King's need for revenue as leverage for prising political concessions from him. As government became more complex and expensive, the Crown's private income and taxation were quite inadequate for government needs. Borrowing from international bankers played an increasingly important part in balancing the national books. Moneylenders were happy to offer loans to the Crown because the potential rewards were enormous. Not only did they earn interest; they might also benefit from royal favour by gaining titles, lands and other perks.

But the risks were correspondingly great. In 1688, the ex-Lord Mayor of London, Sir Robert Viner, suddenly dropped dead, having been worn down by an extravagant royal court unable to maintain interest payments on half a million pounds borrowed from him. And, of course, the tragedy did not end there. Several of Viner's creditors were also ruined. By 1700 parliament had virtually gained control of all the nation's finances. This took the responsibility for income and expenditure away from irresponsible, spendthrift monarchs and placed it in the hands of the Lords and Commons, most of whom were major landowners or merchants. Theoretically, this was a step in the right direction. If you are used to managing a large estate or running a major business you presumably know something about profit and loss and the workings of the money markets. That's fine as long as you are honest and have the public interest at heart. It comes as no surprise to learn that not all eighteenth-century politicians were above corruption and self-interest. Some tended to run the country for the benefit of themselves and their friends.

For a while all went well. Despite heavy expenditure on war, the economy expanded. Merchants prospered. Trade through London virtually doubled during this period. Capital was at a premium and this led, inexorably, to a rapid growth in the number of joint stock companies. The commercial future looked rosy and thousands of people rushed to invest in schemes that 'couldn't fail'. We have seen similar investment booms in our own day. In the 1980s the government sold off nationalised industries and encouraged the shareholder economy. In the 1990s internet trading was all the rage, and millions hurried to take advantage of get-rich-quick schemes they could invest in. Three hundred years ago stocks seemed to offer better prospects than property. Land was, necessarily, a long-term investment and was liable to tax. Shares, on the other hand, could be bought and sold quickly and there was as yet no taxation on unearned income. It seemed to be in everyone's interest, from the government downwards, to encourage dealing on the exchange. Owners, great and small, sold or mortgaged their patrimonial fields in order to rush up to the City with cash in their hot little hands. There they gathered in the coffee houses, where news of the latest flotations was available. And there was no lack of 'advisers' ready to take their money from them.

Enter the stock jobber. It was his task to bring entrepreneurs and investors together and he was a vital cog in the commercial machine. Inventors of burglar alarms or better-quality paper, merchants who had gained important trade concessions, adventurers who believed they could salvage treasure from sunken wrecks – all needed cash to set their enterprises in motion. The jobbers found their working capital for them.

They congregated in Exchange Alley, a triangular maze of narrow streets bounded by Cornhill, Lombard Street and Birchin Lane, to the east of the more respectable commercial heart of the City, where the old-established livery companies and trading bodies, such as the East India Company, had their premises.

They were frowned on by these aristocrats of commerce because they were independent operators and because not a few of them were rogues. Since their activities were unregulated, there was, literally, nothing to stop unscrupulous brokers taking advantage of green investors by offering stock in worthless or even non-existent companies. It was futile for the man gulled out of his savings to seek redress in the courts, for there was no law against obtaining money by false pretences.

This was the springtime of British capitalism and the necessary regulations to protect buyers and sellers had yet to be invented. Sad stories of unwary speculators being ruined and businesses driven into bankruptcy circulated the coffee houses and salons of fashionable London and travelled the turnpike roads to be repeated in wayside inns farther afield – but this did nothing to dampen the ardour of hopeful people eager to climb aboard the investment bandwagon.

As Phineas T. Barnum gratefully observed a century and a half later, 'There's a sucker born every minute'. The general response to tales of woe seems to have been that victims of fraudsters and slick-talking jobbers only had themselves to blame if they were taken in. Those set to follow unfortunates

ROBERT WALPOLE

1720 was the year which established the career of one of Britain's greatest politicians. This 44-year-old Norfolk squire had been a member of the House of Commons since 1701 but it was his ringing denunciation of the South Sea Company's promoters that marked him out as a man of independent and informed judgement. During the months of South Sea frenzy he was dismissed as an unpopular Jeremiah but after the collapse people turned to him as the voice of reason and the obvious person to succeed the disgraced Aislabie as Chancellor of the Exchequer. What few people realised was that Walpole had been a major speculator in the Bubble – one who had had the wit to sell out at the top of the market and make 1000 per cent profit. On the proceeds he built himself the magnificent mansion of Houghton Hall, Norfolk, in the latest Palladian style.

Walpole was a dedicated parliamentarian and remained in office for the next 21 years. He is thought of as the first prime minister, although that title did not exist at the time. He was certainly the first resident of 10 Downing Street, built as the government leader's residence in 1731. Walpole brought stability and common sense to the conduct of government business but he did not neglect his own self-interest. In an age when MPs were not paid, he milked the system for all it was worth by selling offices and using his considerable influence on behalf of suitors who paid him well for his pains. But he spent profligately. At his death in 1745 he was £40,000 in debt (the equivalent of several millions in today's money). It seems he was better at preaching prudence and restraint than in practising it.

down the slippery slope were doubtless convinced 'it could never happen to me'.

By 1711, then, the elements existed for a future scandal on a national scale: (a) a government in sore need of funds, (b) a flourishing trade in commercial stocks, (c) a population who believed that fortunes could easily be made with no effort and very little risk. The government's total borrowing, from several lenders at home and abroad, stood at around £1.2 million and became known as the National Debt.

In 1694, a group of enterprising businessmen had founded the Bank of England, the world's first central bank. This was a very solid institution acting as something between a private bank and a government agency. It tidied up the current situation by taking over the entire government debt for an agreed annual interest payment and the right to issue banknotes. It enjoyed a monopoly of government business and rendered invaluable service in maintaining stability. But there were two problems. The first was that the National Debt continued to rise, largely because of war expenditure. The second was that the bank's charter had a fixed term, eventually extended to 1732, thus encouraging rivals who wanted a piece of this very secure and very lucrative action.

There is one more facet of the situation that must be noted: the slimy world of party politics, and the emergence of one politician in particular, Robert Harley, member of parliament for Herefordshire. A colleague who knew Harley well summed up his character thus:

> …his humour was never to deal clearly or openly, but always with reserve and… simulation; to love tricks even where not

necessary, but from an inward satisfaction he took in applauding his own cunning. If any man was ever born under a necessity of being a knave, he was.

Harley was never popular, even with his own parliamentary colleagues and his career was almost brought to a sudden end before he made his disastrous mark on public policy. On 8 March 1711, he was attacked with a knife by a disgruntled French double agent. The wound was not serious but it temporarily boosted Harley's reputation and made easier the acceptance of his grand design. A few years later, there were thousands of people who heartily wished that the assassination attempt had succeeded.

The early 1700s was the period at which the two-party system was emerging. The Whigs, largely supported by nonconformists and the mercantile interest, had enjoyed power for several years. Harley had begun his political career as a Whig but, sensing the unpopularity of the wars, then put himself at the head of the Tories, the party which drew much of its strength from the High Church and landed elements of the shires.

The election of 1710 brought the Tories to power and Harley (who was created Earl of Oxford in 1711), as Chancellor of the Exchequer, set about reversing the policies of the preceding administration. He rubbished the foreign policy of the Whigs that had kept Britain at war for so long and took delight in exposing the enormous cost of European conflict. He made a blistering attack on the financial arrangements of his rivals. Now the knives were out against the Bank of England. The arrogant leaders of fashionable society hated the bank for its support of the Whigs and because it represented the merchants who rivalled them for wealth and influence.

The hostility of the two groups was a manifestation of the old rivalry between 'land' and 'trade'. The Tories wanted to elbow the Whigs out of the strong position they had gained in the nation's financial life and they wanted to grab for their supporters a sizeable chunk of the profits being made from involvement in government business. This was what lay behind the Chancellor's well-matured plan. What he presented as a master stroke of policy was nothing less than a stratagem to enrich himself and the landed interest. It was a classic example of what can go wrong when the four-in-hand of the national economy is driven by political ambition.

It was on 2 May 1713 that Harley presented his financial scheme to parliament. He and the group of backers he had assembled proposed to set up a commercial enterprise to be known as the South Sea Company. The basis of its operation was to be a monopoly of trade with Spain's South American colonies to be secured by the British government through diplomatic channels as part of the general peace negotiations currently in train at Utrecht.

But the clever twist that made the South Sea Company unique was that the government was to buy into it by exchanging £9 million worth of unfunded National Debt for shares in the new enterprise. Harley had spotted a loophole in the Bank of England's constitution. Its monopoly was protected by Act of Parliament and no other *bank* could take a share in the National Debt but the statute said nothing about excluding trading companies. The prospectus of the South Sea Company, thus, made droolingly attractive reading. On the one hand, trade with the mineral-rich Americas would reap rich rewards and, on the other, the business was rock solid, being virtually underwritten by the government, who would be paying shareholders interest on their investment. To the sceptics all this seemed too good to be true – and, of course, it was.

The Bank of England and their supporters in parliament opposed the scheme. But that did not cause Harley and his collaborators any loss of sleep. They were well able to out-vote any opposition. Furthermore, several of their political enemies were bedazzled by the prospects of huge, easy profits from monopoly trade along the Atlantic seaboard of South and Central America.

For 200 years the Iberians had led Europe in the race to colonise and exploit the lands and peoples of the Americas. Spanish ships had sailed, year in and year out, from the eastward-facing ports of Vera Cruz, Nombre de Dios and Havana bearing gold and silver from the vice-royalties of Peru and New Spain, wealth that had funded Europe's biggest empire. For decades adventurers had been mesmerised by the legend of Eldorado, the ruler of a fabled kingdom of untold riches somewhere in the interior of the vast and still-mysterious continent.

More prosaic, but still commercially important, was the development of plantation agriculture, producing the valuable luxury crops of sugar, tobacco and that novel beverage beloved of the elite – chocolate. But it was not just the prospect of easy access to the exotic exports of the Americas that fired the ambitions of British merchants and investors. The European settlement and colonies of the Caribbean and the North American coastline constituted an important consumer market. The rulers of the New World settlements craved the manufactured necessities of the Old World – cloth, tools, books, weapons, furniture, clothes in the latest fashion and all the paraphernalia of European civilisation which enabled them to maintain a king-like status in their little domains. Fundamental to their way of life was another imported commodity – African slaves. The short life expectancy of plantation labourers meant that there was an insatiable demand for fresh supplies of human cargo. Ever since the mid-sixteenth century this demand had been fed by the cynical cooperation of African chiefs and European captains. Men and women captured in inter-tribal wars or victims of raiding parties were sold to the masters of trading vessels engaged in the lucrative and infamous 'triangular trade' (cheap manufactures from Europe to West Africa; slaves from there to the Americas; plantation products from the colonies back to Europe).

Observers of the political scene thought that the time was opportune for Britain to break into the Iberian trade. By 1700 Spain's empire was crumbling. The government in Madrid was powerless to prevent mercantile interlopers trespassing on their preserves. After years of war, Spain was a nation on its knees. British analysts easily persuaded themselves that the once-great imperial power would be unable to resist determined commercial pressure. Legions of British armchair investors were convinced that the monopoly to be enjoyed by the new company would open up boundless commercial possibilities.

Yet there were some clear-headed commentators at the time, such as the satirist Daniel Defoe, who were not so easily taken in. Defoe was one of the many people fascinated by mariners' tales of travel to exotic lands. In 1719 he had published *The Life and Strange Surprising Adventures of Robinson*

Crusoe. But he was able to keep fact and fiction quite separate in his mind. 'Unless the Spaniards are to be divested of common sense,' he wrote, 'abandoning their own commerce, throwing away the only valuable stake they have left in the world, and in short bent on their own ruin, we cannot suggest that they will ever, on any consideration or for any equivalent, part with so valuable, indeed so inestimable a jewel, as the exclusive power of trade to their own plantations.'

Defoe had put his finger on the fatal flaw in the whole scheme. The much-hyped agreement the British government had negotiated with Spain in 1713 turned out to be very flabby. King Philip V was a proud monarch who was not going to let himself be steam-rollered into a disadvantageous treaty. He was prepared to concede to Harley's company the right to send to the Spanish Main (the mainland coast of the Spanish empire around the Caribbean) one ship a year of moderate tonnage loaded with trade goods, but even on that Philip demanded a 25 per cent tax. The one important concession he did make was a promise to grant Britain the *asiento*. This was the annual contract Spain made for the supply of African slaves. It was normally tendered to the highest bidder but, by the agreement of 1713, the South Sea Company obtained the *asiento* for the next 30 years. This, became known as the 'Earl of Oxford's Masterpiece'.

It would be easier to understand the collapse of 1720 if the South Sea Company had started with a bang. It didn't. Agreement had not been reached with Spain until 1713. Regular trading had not begun until 1717 and had been disrupted the following year by another brief war with Spain. Potential profits were affected by poor marketing strategy. For example, a cargo of woollens, instead of being unloaded at Vera Cruz, where there were plenty of potential customers for it, was put ashore at Cartagena, where there was no demand, and was left to rot in the warehouse. Meanwhile, in London, political in-fighting brought down Robert Harley. At one stage he was impeached for treason and spent a year in the Tower of London. Though acquitted, his political influence was at an end.

How did the South Sea Company survive such reverses? Largely by constantly talking up its supposed potential. Financial markets depend totally on confidence. And in the early eighteenth century everything was on the company's side. Its leaders were uniquely placed to channel and manipulate information. News from the distant Americas took months to reach these shores and ships' captains reported directly to their superiors. They, of course, carefully doctored the details they passed on to shareholders. And the shareholders were eager to be convinced. In the prevailing climate of speculation, customers were queuing to invest. Putting money to use on the exchange became a compelling fashion. Members of the *haut monde* fell over themselves to invest and lesser mortals readily aped them.

Just as the appearance of the modern credit card has fuelled consumer debt, so 300 years ago the profusion of bills of exchange and banknotes made investment easy. As the contemporary poet, Alexander Pope, sourly observed:

> *Blest paper credit! Last and best supply!*
> *That lends Corruption lighter wings to fly!*
> *Gold imp'd by thee, can compass hardest things,*
> *Can pocket States, can fetch or carry Kings;*

A single leaf shall waft an Army o'er,
Or ship off Senates to a distant shore;
A leaf, like Sibyl's, scatter to and fro*
Our fates and fortunes, as the wind shall blow:
Pregnant with thousands flits the Scrap unseen,
And silent sells a King or buys a Queen.

The men upon whose shoulders Harley's mantle had fallen were Robert Knight and John Blunt. These leading spirits of the South Sea Company had all the ambition and self-confidence of John Law with very little of his financial expertise. They were both men of fairly humble origin who, by aggressive business dealing and advantageous marriages, had hauled themselves up into England's governing class. They had formed an alliance with the new Chancellor of the Exchequer, John Aislabie.

Together, these three men went head to head with the Bank of England in a battle for the ultimate prize: the management of the public debt, which now stood at £31 million. The bank and the company made bids and counter-bids to parliament and both sought, by persuasion and bribery, to elicit the votes of members in both houses. The debate was followed eagerly by the country at large. In City coffee houses little else was talked about. The very fact that the Bank of England wanted the same business as the South Sea Company convinced potential investors of the substance – and profitability – of that business. There was much wining and dining of MPs as jobbers and their customers tried to gauge the mood of the assembly. It was a

---

* Sybil was a classical Greek oracle who wrote her prophecies on leaves at the entrance to her cave, whence they were dispersed by the wind.

highly profitable time to be a parliamentarian, with friends, acquaintances and complete strangers ready to pay for inside information and secure promises concerning voting intentions.

With the stakes growing ever higher, the antics of the company directors themselves now plunged headlong over the edge. They paid out between one and two million pounds in bribes. The system they operated was a financial merry-go-round. First they allocated tranches of stock to influential individuals. For example, the Earl of Sunderland, the head of the administration, received £50,000 worth of company shares. Other bribes were presented to members of the government and the royal court. Even the King's female relatives benefited from sweeteners offered by Blunt and Knight to add more social cachet to the company. The recipients, of course, did all they could to ensure the passing of the South Sea Act, in order to enhance the value of their shares. Finally, once the Act had been passed, the directors offered to buy the shares back for cash. They did not lose out because they simply resold the returned shares to new investors on a rising market. It was a win-win situation, or so it must have seemed to those involved in it.

However, the early weeks of 1720, when the supporters of the bank and the company were arguing their case in parliament, were fraught with uncertainty. It was not until 2 February that the Commons decided that the South Sea Company's offer should be accepted and that a bill would be brought in to this effect. Agents and journalists thronging the galleries and corridors of Westminster rushed to the waterside to be rowed down to the City with the news. As a result the value of South Sea shares which had stood at around

£130 (roughly equivalent to the annual income of a modest family) throughout January, leaped to £330 by the end of the day. The boom had begun.

But all was not plain sailing for Blunt, Knight and Co. Several investors wisely took short-term profit and cashed in their shares, which had a flattening effect on their value. It was on 15 February that share dealing in the Mississippi Scheme was suspended in Paris and several British speculators had their fingers burned. It was a warning and company directors worked overtime to counteract it. They needed long-term investors if the public mood was not to change before the necessary legislation had completed its journey through parliament.

There was certainly no lack of warning voices. In the Commons, Robert Walpole, leader of the opposition, lambasted the projectors of the company with ringing oratory. He accused them of playing on the public's gullibility by propagating lies and fantasies. They were, he said, encouraging the British people to indulge in golden dreams of limitless prosperity. The day would come, he warned, when everyone would be rudely awakened and marvel at their own stupidity. He set out his arguments in a pamphlet in an attempt to stem the flow of speculation.

Walpole was quite right about the modus operandi of the company directors. They speculated wildly about the prospects for future growth. As the company elbowed its way into the Americas' trade, untold riches would accrue, they proclaimed. This little-explored region had for generations gripped the public imagination and peopled it with 'lost tribes' rich in precious metals. As Spain's grip on these lands weakened, South Sea operatives would be poised to take over their position. As is invariably the case, when presented with competing prophecies, people believed what they wanted to believe. When Walpole, who enjoyed a long reputation as a fine speaker, rose from his seat in the Commons chamber, several members walked out.

The South Sea Act was signed and passed into law on 7 April. Its impact in the City was like the breaching of a dam. Caution had held back thousands of potential investors. Now they rushed to buy. Clamouring crowds clogged Exchange Alley. Traffic in Cornhill came to a standstill because of the number of carriages conveying their owners to the jobbers' shops. Ballad writers lampooned the madness that now possessed normally sober citizens:

Then stars and garters did appear*
Among the meaner rabble;
To buy and sell, to see and hear
The Jews and Gentiles squabble.

Many great ladies thither came
And plied in chariots daily,
Or pawned their jewels for a sum
To venture in the Alley.

The simple facts of the sad summer of 1720 can easily be told, but behind them lies a wretched, tangled web of lost fortunes and ruined lives.

On 20 May share values broke through the £500 barrier. The boost was partly provided by overseas investors, for Britain was not alone in catching the shareholding bug. The

* Knights of the Garter, the cream of respectable society.

collapse of the Mississippi Scheme, far from warning continental brokers off such ventures, left them looking for other
homes for their clients' cash. The South Sea Company was
one of the enterprises that benefited from the market surge.
But it was at home that frenzy turned into mania. As ordinary people saw the paper profits that were being made, they
panicked at the prospect of being left behind. Solid citizens
became convinced that they owed it, if not to themselves,
then to their children to grab this once-in-a-lifetime opportunity.

By mid-June the share price was nudging £800. The
people who were now being sucked into the South Sea
maelstrom were, by and large, those who did not understand
the mechanics of the stock exchange. They were ignorant
of the golden rule that it is folly to buy on a rising market.
Others who had got in reasonably early hung on in the hope
that their profit would increase still further.

The dramatist, John Gay, plunged all his not-inconsid-
erable income from writing into South Sea, saw his principal rise to £20,000, but declined to cash in his shares in
the summer and lost everything. It was some years before he
recovered financial stability by writing the immensely popular *The Beggar's Opera.*

Wiser, more experienced investors chose their moment to
pull out. They grasped the fact that, as one analyst said, 'The
additional rise of this stock above the true capital will be only
imaginary. One added to one, by any rules of vulgar arithme-
tic, will never make three and a half. Consequently, all the fic-
titious value must be a loss to some persons... The only way
to prevent it to oneself must be to sell out betimes and let the
devil take the hindmost.' Many of the lucky or clever ones

A certain Good Old Worthy Rich in Lands,
Keeping his Servants Wages in his Hands,
Bought South Sea Stock, when they knew nothing o
Sold it when High, and gave to them the Profit.

ONE LAMPOONIST PRODUCED A SET OF PLAYING CARDS TO
ILLUSTRATE HUMAN FOLLY, EACH WITH A DIFFERENT
PICTURE AND CAUTIONARY RHYME

who followed that advice flaunted their new-found wealth. Like 1980s yuppies in their Porsches and designer clothes, they wore their money on their sleeves. Carriage builders were kept busy designing impressive equipages. Tailors and dressmakers could scarcely keep up with their orders. Property prices went through the roof as the nouveau-riche fell over themselves to buy town houses and country estates. The directors of the company were lauded as public heroes. Blunt's name appeared on the honours list and he was awarded a baronetcy 'for his extraordinary services in raising public credit to a height not known before'.

Yet, beneath the euphoria and public acclaim, those responsible for the boom were anxious. Because the value of the company bore no relationship to the total face value of shares, its leaders had to keep talking it up. They needed a constant inflow of funds to outweigh the effect of profit-taking. If shares were allowed to regress to something approaching their true worth, the resulting loss of confidence could only lead to a crash. They, therefore, went on making stock allocations, paying dividends and instructing their agents to buy.

Nowadays we would call this systematic accounting fraud, the kind of crime that Enron was guilty of in 2000 when it boosted its market value by claiming revenue of $111 billion. Strictly speaking, by the criminal codes of the day, what the promoters of the South Sea Company and their political aiders and abettors were doing was not illegal. Corrupt and immoral, certainly. Incompetent, without doubt. But not an infringement of any statute law. The South Sea Company was not in essence a scam. Those who had originated it had believed that it was viable. They simply got caught up in the coils of their own enthusiasm.

The same could not be said of many of the spivs who took advantage of the prevailing overheated stock market to launch their own dubious schemes. Their activities and the havoc they created in the life of modest investors was, in some ways, more unpalatable than the blowing of the South Sea Bubble. They demonstrated just how deep were the roots of uncontrolled capitalism.

Although the price of South Sea stock had gone beyond the reach of most, people were eager to invest in something – anything. And in response, the jobbers on Exchange Alley hawked shares in a kaleidoscope of crazy ventures: everything from trading in hair and insuring employers against the dishonesty of servants, to extracting silver from lead. But the most ludicrous of all these projects was a company founded to carry on 'an undertaking of great advantage but nobody is to know what it is'. The originator of that particular confidence trick opened his office for one day, took £2,000 from gullible investors and promptly disappeared.

Blunt and King were alarmed by the flourishing of this nefarious underworld because it threatened to bring their own operation into disrepute and because it siphoned off funds which might, otherwise, have come their way. They urged their parliamentary friends to inhibit the proliferation of swindles – and incredibly got their way. The result was an Act, later dubbed the 'Bubble Act', which restricted the incorporation of new joint stock companies. It became law on 9 June. By then, however, the damage had been done.

On 26 June South Sea stock reached its peak – £1,050

per share. It was no longer possible to boost confidence artificially, especially when Blunt and other directors, unable to resist making a killing, cashed in their own holdings. The fall was gradual at first, partly because fashionable London decamped to its country estates in high summer. By early July the price was around £900 but it lost another hundred points before the end of the month.

Now all was confusion and recrimination at the company's headquarters. Directors were being attacked in the street and Blunt was threatened with assassination. His nephew, Charles, another member of the board, cut his throat. The great crash finally came in September. Share values plummeted from £750 to £200. The company principals had not the slightest idea what to do. 'The company have yet come to no determination,' wrote one observer, 'for they are in such a wood that they know not which way to turn. By several gentlemen lately come to town I perceive the very name of a South Sea man grows abominable in every country.'

At last all Blunt and his colleagues could do was go cap-in-hand to the Bank of England and beg to be bailed out. What grim satisfaction that must have given the company's old rivals. But the bank was in no position to dip into its reserves, for the very good reason that it had none, or certainly none to spare. Like the entire financial sector, it was in difficulties.

The crisis had caused a run on gold, and the bank, as it desperately called in loans and shipped bullion from wherever it could be found, now came close to shutting its doors in the face of its depositors. One customer presenting £8,000 worth of paper money for redemption was obliged to accept it in shillings and sixpences, approximately 150,000 coins.

In the end, however, the bank managed to pull back from the brink. It was able to keep its head above water and, in the last days of the year, Robert Walpole, instead of smugly saying 'told you so', brokered a deal between the two institutions that saved the South Sea Company from total extinction. By this time the value of South Sea stock had returned to about £130 a share, the level at which it had been at the very beginning of its dramatic switchback ride.

1720 had been an appalling year and not just for the few thousand people who had invested directly in the South Sea Company. Banks folded. Businesses went bankrupt. Property owners were forced into negative equity when artificially inflated prices tumbled again. Ambitious building projects came to an abrupt halt. Workers were laid off. Elderly people lost their life savings in tin-pot, catch-penny schemes. The debtors' prisons had never been so full.

The bursting of the South Sea Bubble, thus, made an enormous impact. Just how enormous we can gauge from the quantity of comments left to us by contemporary observers. Caricaturists, preachers, dramatists, journalists, songwriters, painters and poets – all were moved to record their thoughts on the tragedy.

> *At length, corruption, like a general flood,*
> *Did deluge all; and avarice creeping on,*
> *Spread, like a low-borne mist and hid the sun.*
> *Statesmen and patriots plied alike the stocks,*
> *Peeress and butler shared alike the box;*
> *And judges jobbed and bishops hit the town,*

And mighty dukes packed cards for half-a-crown:
Britain was sunk in lucre's sordid charms.

So Alexander Pope moralised. Less elegant were the re-
frains of popular ballad-mongers:

A bubble is blown up in air,
On which fine prospects do appear;
The bubble breaks, the prospect's lost,
Yet must some bubble pay the cost.
Hubble Bubble; all is smoke,
Hubble Bubble, all is broke,
Farewell your houses, lands and flocks,
For all you have is now in stocks.

Some journalists were more inclined to sympathy for those
facing ruin and disgrace:

To imprison an undone gentleman or a ruined tradesman
NOW; or to keep them confined that are already shut up, is
it not like murdering those that are sick of the plague? The
distemper has been a visitation; South Sea has been a judgement from heaven. Shall we not pity them whom God has
smitten?

One enterprising lampoonist sought to leave posterity a
more permanent record of human folly by producing a set
of playing cards, each with a different picture and cautionary
rhyme. The six of clubs recalled:

A famous builder of meridian Coaches,
To make each South Sea drab appear a duchess
Had forty coaches at one time bespoke,

But falling stock did thirty-five revoke.

The jack of hearts told another sad tale:

A South Sea lady having much improved
Her fortune, proudly slighted him she loved,
But South Sea falling, sunk her fortune low.
She would have had him then but he cried, 'No!'

On the five of clubs a conference of three doctors presented an overview. They discussed various cures for the South Sea sickness, including incarceration in the Bedlam madhouse.

But all agreed the fools should still endure it
Till smarting poverty alone should cure it.

The scandal actually helped to launch the career of one of the great geniuses of the eighteenth century. William Hogarth's first published print was a vivid denunciation not of the South Sea schemers but of the evils of society that had enabled them to blow their bubble. His acid pen depicted Self Interest breaking Honesty on a wheel, Villainy flogging Honour and Trade reduced to destitution. His caption pointed up the moral in a few words: 'So much for money's magic powers'. It is Hogarth who, as so often, gets to the heart of the matter. The most debilitating result of this monumental scandal was the blow to the national psyche.

In Oxfordshire John Churchill, Duke of Marlborough, was building a monumental mansion called Blenheim Palace with money given to him by the government. This was the gesture of a grateful nation for the stupendous victories Churchill had won in the recent wars. Buoyed up by military

success, Britain's reputation had never stood higher – until the crisis of 1720. The South Sea Bubble delivered national self-confidence a blow so great it would be several decades before it recovered.

What Happened Before...

1783   ROTTENEST YEAR

...And What Came After

1783

BEWARE OF HISTORIANS! We fiddle with the past. We tell you what we think is important. What we believe you ought to know.

Older readers may have had their earliest knowledge of history shaped by books such as *Our Island Story*, whose pages are filled with a cavalcade of glorious achievement from Agincourt to Trafalgar, peopled by great men like Drake, Shakespeare and Brunel. The aim of such 'histories' was to instil in young minds pride in being British. Modern, more politically correct historians go to the other extreme. They want us to beat our breasts over the iniquities of slavery, the denial of equal opportunities to women or the stultifying influence of class. Of course, all this is distortion.

More objective academic historians fall into a different trap, seeking to impress upon us what they believe to be 'significant'. They concentrate on personalities who stood head and shoulders above their contemporaries and events that left a permanent mark on human affairs. In their eagerness to explore, as fairly as possible, the grand themes of international rivalries, social change, technological advance and political development, they avert their eyes from the 'trivial', the 'insignificant'. But, again and again, it is the trivial which lends a given moment its significance – the trivial which may not have made a lasting mark in the grand sweep of history, but that made a great and immediate impact on ordinary people's lives.

Take, for instance, 1783. It was the year the USA broke free from Britain. It was the year William Pitt became prime minister at the age of 24 and went on to lead the country for most of the next 23 years. And it was the year of the great dry fog. The what? Exactly. You have probably never heard of the extraordinary meteorological phenomena of 1783-4 that impacted on the life of every man, woman and child in the country. To the people of the time these things mattered enormously. But were they 'significant'? Only if you believe, as I do, that anything that sheds light on human behaviour is significant. We'll get back to the fog shortly. First, let's look at the better recorded events which plunged the nation into humiliation, gloom and political chaos.

Britain had spent the middle years of the eighteenth century building a global empire. Its armies and navies had established their supremacy over European rivals and indigenous rulers from North America and the Caribbean islands to India. London merchants built fortunes on long-distance voyages to trading posts in China and the East Indies. The economy worked by supplying slaves from Africa to the New World plantations and by exporting cloth and manufactured goods from our 'dark Satanic mills' to our trading partners round the world. In exchange we imported silk, porcelain, tea and other luxuries to grace the mansions of the *nouveaux riches.* Thanks to the National Trust and private owners we can still visit many of these impressive houses and gain some idea of how vital imported exotica were in this age of conspicuous consumption. As we admire the Ming vases, the embroidered silk panels, the tables laid out with dinner services brought all the way from Canton or copied in the factories of the ingenious Mr Wedgwood, we gain some idea of what it was like for the privileged few who sat at the centre of a commercial web that stretched right round the globe. Britain's North American colonies were indispensable pieces in the commercial jigsaw. As the settlers on the eastern seaboard worked their way westwards, subduing the indigenous peoples and appropriating their tribal homelands, they needed the pots and pans and knives and tools and calico and woollens and tea the mother country turned out in abundance or brought in from other parts of the empire. It was vital that the colonists were kept dependent on Britain's factories and merchant marine and that they paid taxes for the privilege of being part of the greatest trading enterprise the world had ever seen.

In 1776, some of those upstart colonists had had the effrontery to try to cut their land adrift from the British Empire. King George III was passionate about teaching his ungrateful subjects a lesson. As the War of American Independence dragged on without a clear victory; as the burden of taxation to pay for it grew; and as stories of military incompetence travelled back to Britain; the conflict became increasingly unpopular. George III and his Prime Minister, Lord North, took the brunt of the criticism, principally delivered through the popular caricaturists of the day. When France entered the war on the side of the colonists, the military balance tilted in favour of the Americans. The surrender of the main British army at Yorktown in October 1781 marked the effective end of hostilities and representatives gathered in Paris for peace talks.

This humiliating defeat and the inevitability of negotiating with the 'rebels' threw the British political machine into chaos. Conflicting policies and rival ambitions made government virtually unworkable. Throughout 1782-3 ministers rose and fell. The King parted company with Lord North, accusing him of 'treachery and ingratitude of the blackest nature'. He seriously contemplated abdicating. North resigned in March. He was replaced as prime minister by Lord Rockingham with the pro-American Charles James Fox as foreign minister. When Rockingham died after only four months in office, Fox refused to serve under the King's nominee, Lord Shelburne. Shady backstairs dealings resulted in Fox joining with North to bring down Shelburne (February 1783). It was a cynical combination of political opposites entered into purely to gain power. Other parliamentarians mistrusted it, as did the nation. For his part, King George called it 'the most unprincipled coalition the annals of this or any other nation can equal'. He felt a fierce personal loathing for Fox. The politician angered his sovereign, not only with his radical politics, but also with his habit of carousing with the weak-willed Prince of Wales and, in the opinion of the King, corrupting the morals of the heir to the throne. One of the first things the new administration did was vote in a large increase in the personal allowance of the Prince of Wales. George gained his revenge in December. An important bill sponsored by Fox was sent up to the Lords for their votes. The King made it clear that anyone who supported the measure would forfeit his favour and, therefore, be socially ostracised. But even with this broadest of hints the bill was only narrowly defeated in the upper house.

And while all this was going on at Westminster, Britain's representatives in Paris were trying to make a peace treaty with the nation which now called itself the United States of America. There were many of King George's subjects who shared his belief that Britain should not be sitting round a table with the ex-colonists discussing the abandonment of what was potentially the largest and most promising component of the British Empire. Despite the recent military reverses, Britain still controlled New York, Detroit, Charleston and several other key towns. It had supremacy at sea. The colonial army was exhausted and unable to maintain its position without French support. If independence was to be recognised, several issues would have to be sorted out, such as compensation for those Americans who had fought for the mother country and also for British merchants whose stocks had been confiscated by the rebels in American ports at the beginning of the conflict. But Britain was diplomatically isolated, branded by other nations as an oppressive colonial power. It had to take the best terms it could get. The basic details of a treaty with America had been thrashed out by the end of 1782 but could not be ratified until agreements had been reached with France, Spain and Holland, who also had interests in the New World, and were hoping to take full advantage of Britain's humiliation by carving off pieces of its empire for themselves. Territory in North America, the West Indies and as far away as India was up for grabs, not to mention Gibraltar, which Spain was desperate to regain. These tricky negotiations were not helped by instability at Britain's political centre.

The country was, now more than ever before, at the mercy of men governed by personal hatreds and ambitions. What happened in those December days strained the constitution to its limits. Members of the House of Commons were outraged that the King should interfere so blatantly in the workings of parliament. They passed a motion to that effect. George went further. He dismissed the entire cabinet without even doing them the courtesy of informing them of his decision in a private audience. But, as always in politics, it was what went on behind the scenes that really mattered. The movers and shakers were in their element, forging intrigues and plots, offering deals and bribes, carefully doing their sums as they assembled support for a change of administration. Their principal asset was the unpopularity of both North and Fox. Their problem was finding a new team to lead the government. Was there anyone available who had the stature to command without being tainted by corruption and incompetence?

The only person who could be found was a politically inexperienced 24-year-old lawyer who was MP for Appleby, Cumberland. His name was William Pitt and he had served briefly under Shelburne. He had some reputation as an effective Commons orator and he prided himself on being independent and having no party allegiance. But Pitt's main claim to fame was that he was the son of the Earl of Chatham (often known as 'Pitt the Elder'), one of the leading politicians of the preceding generation. In March 1783, when the King was desperately casting around for new talent, Pitt turned down a request to take office, deciding to concentrate on his legal practice. However, in the confusion of the following December, when the King called upon him a second time, Pitt accepted and was appointed as prime minister and chancellor of the exchequer. If ever there was a poisoned chalice, this was it. No-one expected Pitt to survive long in office and few politicians of stature were prepared to hitch their fortunes to his. As one contemporary put it, he 'hastily patched together an administration composed of men wholly inadequate to the work before them'. He could find no-one in the Commons worthy of government office so his cabinet was entirely made up of peers. The young Prime Minister, therefore, had to face the taunts of Fox and his allies in the lower house alone. For the next few months his position was precarious in the extreme. His only mainstay was the King, who looked on Pitt as his salvation from the men he hated. Only Fox's mounting unpopularity in the country at large, resulting in his defeat in the general election of March 1784, saved Pitt's bacon and enabled him to return to parliament with a workable majority.

You can read all about the chronic political chaos of 1782-4 in the history books. But what you won't find there is any reference to the dry fog which afflicted the whole country for much of this time and was a far greater and more distressing everyday experience than the antics of the politicians in Westminster. These days we are accustomed to hearing a great deal about global warming and carbon footprints but, of course, to our ancestors two and a half centuries ago, such terms would have had no meaning whatsoever. To them it would have seemed impossible that man, a mere creation by God, could, by his own actions, decide the fate of the planet.

So, when dreadful 'signs and portents' appeared in the heavens, people looked for supernatural explanations.

> …The bursts of thunder and lightning, or rather sheets of flame, were without intermission. Those that were asleep in the town were waked and many thought the day of judgement was come.

This was the scene that confronted the travelling evangelist and founder of Methodism, the Reverend John Wesley, when he visited Witney in Oxfordshire, a town in panic, in the summer of 1783.

> Men, women and children flocked out of their houses and kneeled down together in the streets. With the flames the grace of God came down also in a manner never known before; and as the impression was general, so it was lasting: It did not pass away with the storm; but the spirit of seriousness, with that of grace and supplication, continued… On Sunday morning, before the usual time of service, the church was quite filled. Such a sight was never seen in that church before… I preached in the evening at Wood-Green, where a multitude flocked together, on the Son of Man coming in his glory. The word fell heavy upon them, and many of their hearts were as melting wax…

We might dismiss such behaviour as the result of superstition or a reaction to emotionally charged, exploitative preaching. But, then, we have not seen what our ancestors saw in that frightening year – meteorological phenomena that were as disturbing as they were inexplicable. In 1783-4 the people of Britain were facing not only political meltdown but annihilation. As an anonymous poet wrote:

...when of the late impetuous floods of flame
In red confusion burst, and rolling came
Tremendous peals of thunder, then with dread
Shudder'd and look'd aghast each guilty head.

A nation already experiencing low morale was now visited by something far worse than the loss of overseas territory; something which beset all of its inhabitants, from the most elevated in society to the lowliest:

> ...Besides the alarming meteors and tremendous thunderstorms that affrighted and distressed the different counties of this kingdom, the peculiar haze, or smoky fog, that prevailed for many weeks in this island... was a most extraordinary appearance, unlike anything known within the memory of man...
>
> The sun at noon looked as blank as a clouded moon, and shed a rust-coloured ferruginous light on the ground, and floors of rooms; but was particularly lurid and blood-coloured at rising and setting. All the time the heat was so intense that butchers' meat could hardly be eaten on the day after it was killed; and flies so swarmed in the lanes and hedges that they rendered the horses half frantic, and riding irksome
>
> The country people began to look with a superstitious awe at the red, lowering aspect of the sun; and indeed there was reason for the most enlightened person to be apprehensive.

So wrote the Reverend Gilbert White who lived almost the whole of his life in his native village of Selborne, Hampshire, and devoted himself to observing and recording the details of the changing seasons. He eventually published his amateur scientific records as *The Natural History of Selborne*. In 1783 White was approaching the end of a long life, so when he referred to the climatic disaster of that year as 'unlike anything known within the memory of man' he knew what he was talking about.

But we don't have to rely upon the reminiscences of one man. The poet, William Cowper, living in Huntingdon, explained to a friend:

> So long in a country not subject to fogs, we have been cover'd with one of the thickest I remember. We never see the sun but shorn of his beams, the trees are scarce discernable at a mile's distance, he sets with the face of a hot salamander and rises with the same complexion.

Before the freak conditions appeared in June, Britain and Europe were already experiencing their hottest summer on record. Violent storms, like the one which shook the people of Witney, were frequent. Now, the sudden masking of the sun produced a severe drop in temperature. Frost and ice were reported in several places, and this in the month of June. William Gilpin, a writer who travelled widely throughout the country, referred to the unprecedented summer phenomenon as a 'dry fog' and that became the standard description of whatever it was that permeated the whole of the country from Land's End to John O' Groats.

This meteorological anomaly was not just an intriguing phenomenon to be recorded by gentlemen who had the leisure to write about it. It was a terrible visitation that affected all vegetation. Leaves withered, crops failed, insects died in their millions, preventing the pollination of fruit and flowers:

'THE PECULIAR HAZE, OR SMOKY FOG, THAT PREVAILED FOR MANY
WEEKS IN THIS ISLAND... WAS A MOST EXTRAORDINARY APPEARANCE,
UNLIKE ANYTHING KNOWN WITHIN THE MEMORY OF MAN...

...the land offered an aspect of severe devastation, the green
colour of plants had disappeared and everywhere the leaves
were dry, just as in October or November... This affected a
wide variety of plants: some were covered in spots, others
changed gradually while some leaves dried up completely...
the fall of leaves that summer caused many fruits to fail for
lack of nourishment... On Wednesday June 25th it was first
observed here, and in this neighbourhood, that all the different species of grain, viz wheat, barley, and oats, were very
yellow, and in general to have had all their leaves – but their
upper ones in particular – withered within two or three inch-
es at their ends...

Animals also suffered. The first impact was on their food

supply. According to a Cambridge newspaper:

> The grazing land, which only the day before was full of juice and had upon it the most delightful verdure, did, immediately after this uncommon event, look as if it had been dried up by the sun, and was to walk on like hay. The beans were turned to a whitish colour, the leaf and blade appearing as if dead.

But the stock in the fields soon had other afflictions to contend with. Sores and bare patches appeared on their skin. There were stories of some being felled by giant hailstones.

It is not difficult to imagine the result of all this rural disruption on food supplies and prices. By the autumn of 1783, grain was being sold at 30 per cent more than its pre-fog price. This sparked protests and riots. At Halifax market men gathered from the surrounding weaving villages. Led by Thomas Spencer, an ex-soldier, the mob forced merchants to sell wheat and oats at the old prices. This scene was being played out elsewhere in the country and mobs even blockaded ports to prevent producers exporting grain in order to achieve higher prices.

People, especially agricultural workers, did not escape the fog. William Cowper reported:

> Such multitudes are indisposed by fevers in this country that farmers have difficulty gathering their harvest, the labourers having been almost every day carried out of the field incapable of work and many die.

Men, women and children found breathing unpleasant and difficult. Many suffered from respiratory complaints, eye irritation and violent headaches. The death rate rose dramatically. All over the country there were roughly twice as many deaths in 1783 as in preceding and succeeding years. There were two mortality peaks: one in late summer, the other in January-February 1784. Whatever it was that visited the land in these dreadful months carried off some 23,000 souls. Small wonder that the people looked to the skies expecting to see the four horsemen of the Apocalypse. Again it was Cowper who recorded:

> Some fear to go to bed, expecting an earthquake; some declare that the sun neither rises nor sets where he did, and assert with great confidence that the day of judgement is at hand.

Others saw a diabolical hand in the heavenly disturbances and called upon their parish clergy to carry out exorcisms.

Setting aside epidemics, the dry fog was the most deadly natural phenomenon ever to hit Britain. But observers did not automatically link the wave of death and sickness to it. For all they knew, the country was suffering a double scourge – portents in earth and sky *and* a new kind of pestilence. Fearing the outbreak of some kind of plague, the government even made plans to close all the ports.

It was a terrible visitation that affected all vegetation. Leaves withered, crops failed, and insects died in their millions, preventing the pollination of fruit and flowers.

The fog which appeared in late June and only dissipated slowly throughout the autumn was part of a sequence of unusual events. It was preceded, as we have seen, by the hottest summer on record, accompanied by violent storms. Among the 'horrible manifestations' noted by Gilbert White was an abnormal number of wasps. Then came the alarming foggy late summer and autumn. This was followed by the coldest winter on record, with temperatures consistently two degrees Celsius below the norm. Selbourne experienced 28 days of continuous frost. More sea ice was observed around the coasts than ever witnessed before or since.

The scientific knowledge did not exist which might have enabled experts to establish what connections, if any, there were between these different phenomena. But this did not prevent naturalists offering their own theories – theories which did not depend on religious explanations. This was the age of the European Enlightenment, an explosion of scientific and philosophical enquiry whose exponents were intent on blowing away old ideas and superstitions and asserting pure reason as the only reliable guide for humanity adrift in the universe.

One French astronomer declared confidently that the disturbing events were nothing more than the results of strong sunlight after a prolonged period of heavy rain. Some of his colleagues in Paris flew a kite to a very high altitude and were puzzled to discover that it returned to earth covered with tiny black insects. Yet it was in Paris that one of the great figures of the Enlightenment began to draw together the evidence on which some explanation of the dry fog and its attendant phenomena could be based. Benjamin Franklin, as well as being one of the signatories of the American Declaration of Independence and his country's representative in France, was an experimental scientist with an irresistibly inquisitive mind. As all scientists should, he preceded theory with clear observation and recording of facts:

> During several of the summer months of the year 1783, when the effect of the sun's rays to heat the earth in these northern regions should have been greater, there existed a constant fog over all Europe, and a great part of North America. This fog was of a permanent nature; it was dry, and the rays of the sun seemed to have little effect towards dissipating it, as they easily do a moist fog, arising from water. They were, indeed, rendered so faint in passing through it, that when collected in the focus of a burning glass they would scarce kindle brown paper. Of course, their summer effect of heating the Earth was exceedingly diminished. Hence the surface was early frozen. Hence the first snows remained on it unmelted, and received continual additions. Hence the air was more chilled, and the winds more severely cold. Hence perhaps the winter of 1783-4 was more severe than any that had happened for many years. The cause of this universal fog is not yet ascertained…

What Franklin established was that the remarkable events of 1783-4 were experienced over a very wide area. Much of the northern hemisphere was affected. From North America, Scandinavia, Russia, France, Holland, Germany, Switzerland, Italy and north Africa came similar stories of a sulphurous haze, defoliation of vegetation and human mortality. This led Franklin to venture a theory that might be tested: could the fog have been due to the 'vast quantity of smoke, long continuing, to issue during the summer from Hecla in Iceland, and that other volcano

THE 18TH CENTURY PAPARAZZI

The late eighteenth century had its own equivalent to today's paparazzi. They were the caricaturists, men who made their living by social and political muck-raking. It was around 1783 that their trade took off. At that time three rival print-makers had newly established London shops. Crowds could daily be seen gathered round the windows of William Humphrey in the Strand, Samuel Fores in Piccadilly and William Holland in Drury Lane. Displayed for sale were cheap prints – produced by back-room hacks – from the designs of a handful of artists who became celebrities in their own right.

The most famous (or notorious) of these popular artists was James Gillray (1757-1815) whose career took off in 1782 with a series of very explicit images of the adulteries of prominent socialites, Sir Richard and Lady Worsley. Thereafter Gillray's pen spared no-one. He depicted the King farting, clergy consorting with whores, politicians as hellish demons and sexual goings-on in high places.

Gillray – a misogynistic manic depressive who eventually went into mental decline – and the other leading caricaturists got away with publishing pictures which today would be considered libellous and pornographic. But, of course, they could be successful only because some of society's leaders were open to being lampooned and because the public at large took salacious pleasure in seeing their 'betters' exposed.

THE DEVONSHIRE, or Most Approved Method of Securing Votes

GILLRAY'S PEN SPARED NO ONE..

that arose out of the sea near that island'?

Right location; wrong volcano. Iceland was remote from the regular commercial traffic lanes along which news flowed. Therefore, it took several months for information about the tragedy that had overwhelmed that island to become more widely known. Iceland is a country well accustomed to volcanic activity. Laki, in the southern part of the island, is just one of several centres. And on 3 June 1783, a long fissure had opened up there and begun spewing lava and volcanic ash from 130 small craters. This was not the kind of explosion the word 'volcano' usually conjures up in our minds. Laki was not a cone propelling white-hot magma and gases thousand of metres into the sky. It was less dramat-ic – but no less devastating. The lava flow caused compara-tively little damage. But the clouds of sulphur dioxide and fluorine were deadly. During the five months of this eruption some 120 million tons of toxic gases were pumped into the atmosphere. That is three times the average annual industrial pollution of the whole of modern Europe. It was this that created the choking haze and nauseous, sulphurous stench. Worse than that, in the lower atmosphere sulphur dioxide dissolved in water vapour to produce sulphurous acid which then fell as acid rain. The impact on Iceland's flora and fauna was catastrophic and Laki claimed the lives of a quarter of the island's population.

The wider implications would not have been so serious had the eruption not coincided with unusual meteorologi-cal conditions. The hot summer of 1783 was the result of an almost stationary anticyclone covering much of northern Europe. The airs were light. The winds that would normally have wafted the dry fog northwards into the unpopulated Arctic were absent. So the ashen cloud simply spread. The Paris correspondent for the *Bristol Journal* informed the pa-per's readers on 19 July:

For a considerable time past the weather has been very re-markable here; a kind of hot fog obscures the atmosphere, and gives the sun much of a dull red appearance which the wintry fogs sometimes produce… those who are come lately from Rome say, that it is as thick and hot in Italy, and that even the top of the Alps is covered with it, and letters from Spain affirm the same.

I don't suppose it was any consolation to the inhabitants of

Bristol to know that their suffering was being shared by the French, Spaniards and Italians.

Laki erupted ten times between June and October and the noxious cloud was continually replenished throughout that time. A particularly distressing aspect of the death toll it caused was the fact that the worst affected were often the younger and fitter within the community. Because they laboured in the fields or were occupied in other outdoor jobs they were most exposed to the stifling atmosphere.

Eventually the fog dissipated. But Laki had not finished its deadly work. Volcanic gases lurking in the atmosphere continued to divert the sun's rays, bringing about 'global cooling' and the bad winter of 1783-4. Analyses of tree rings in parts of Russia suggest that in the early months of 1784 temperatures hit their lowest levels for centuries. If accurate records were available we might well discover that the situation in Britain was almost as dramatic. The dry fog came as such a shock to the people of Britain because in our temperate zone we are unaccustomed to such freak conditions. The people of sub-Saharan Africa get famine-inducing droughts. Monsoon floods are frequent in southern Asia. Those who live on the Caribbean fringe have to put up with annual hurricanes. Forest fires sometimes ravage sun-parched areas of Australia. But bad-tempered weather of that nature is not what we pay our taxes for. And what our ancestors got was a taste of what happens when the atmosphere becomes poisoned.

For them the extraordinary weather of 1783-4 remained unexplained. Franklin got closer to the answer than anyone and there were a few other scientists who agreed with his analysis. But no-one could prove that the volcanic theory was correct. Only in recent years has painstaking research by specialists made it possible to unravel the mystery of the dry fog. So, a mystery it remained for those who lived through it. But the traumatic year of the dry fog passed. The world did not come to an end. Normal weather patterns gradually returned. This largely explains why historians have not recorded this disaster. That and the fact that the last quarter of the eighteenth century was dominated by major political events. Six years after the plenipotentiaries of several nations had met in Paris to put an end to the War of American Independence, that city would witness the outbreak of the French Revolution. Shrieking mobs would range the streets calling for the blood of their oppressors and demanding a constitution like that of the United States of America which would guarantee them 'liberty, equality and freedom'. Soon revolutionary courts were sending the King and thousands of his wealthier subjects to the guillotine. Pitt's government could not remain bystanders. Britain was sucked into war, a war which would rage, on and off, for the next twenty-five years.

These are the events that have most engaged the minds and dominated the writings of historians. Some writers who do give space to the economic results of meteorological disturbance have actually related them to the French Revolution, seeing the agricultural disruption as one factor in the growing resentment of the people that eventually exploded in 1789. It is as though the widespread distress of 1783-4 only matters in terms of its connection with events we have already decided are 'significant'. Well, as the song says, it ain't necessarily so!

That's why I suggest we should beware of historians.

The narrative of human affairs is not just one of 'significant' events that have to be linked together. We need to be aware of the relevance and the relative importance of events *for those who lived through them*. It would be absurd to deny that 23,000 deaths and the breakdown in health of an unknown number of people were not important on the grounds that no-one understood their cause or because they did not change the world or because they do not fit into a pattern of 'historical development'. 1783 is a year to be contemplated for its own sake. It was an awful year to live through.

What Happened Before...

1812-3   ROTTENEST YEAR

...And What Came After

1812–3

WHEN MR BINGLEY wanted to please his beloved Jane by enabling her to see more of her sister, Elizabeth Darcy, he simply 'bought an estate in a neighbouring county to Derbyshire'. Jane Austen's characters were fictional but modelled on the highest echelons of English society. Conspicuous consumption was as natural to the Regency upper classes as it is to the overpaid footballers and film stars of the 21st century. No-one regards Posh and Becks as typical of modern society today or even as inhabitants of the *real* world. It would be equally misguided to think that Mr Bingley and Mr Darcy represented the kind of life that most British people were familiar with in 1812. The glittering ballrooms of Pemberley or Rosings were certainly very far from the experience of most ordinary people in Britain, who lived hard lives in rat-infested rural hovels or houses crammed among the 'dark Satanic mills' of new industrial towns. The reality was that, as Austen looked out from her cottage at Chawton and drew inspiration from the peaceful Hampshire fields, Britain was falling apart.

The signs were obvious to anyone who picked up a newspaper or ventured too far from the more fashionable city streets. When John Nash, the architect, drew up in 1812 the plans which he set before parliament the following year for a new London thoroughfare, to be called Regent Street, he declared that his intention was 'that the new street should cross the eastern entrance to all the streets occupied by the higher classes and to leave out to the east all the bad streets'. His vision was for a ghettoised capital where artisans, apprentices, labourers and the 'indigent poor' could be kept in their overcrowded, foul-smelling neighbourhoods, well away from the carefully policed boroughs frequented by the upper classes. But it was not only crime and cholera that were spawned in the cheap drinking dens and bagnios that abounded between Soho and Holborn; the contagion of sedition and rebellion was spreading at a rate that sent the authorities into a panic.

Nor was London the only city where various hazards were part of daily life. For example, the good citizens of Edinburgh were terrorised by a bunch of teenagers calling themselves the Keelie Gang. Before the year was out, three of the ringleaders had been hanged for murder, robbery with violence and affray and five transported to penal colonies in Australia.

In the smaller towns of the north and the Midlands, where the industrial revolution in the textile industries had put hundreds of handloom workers out of business, organised mobs prowled the streets, breaking into factories to smash machines and power looms. They threatened mill owners and gunned down profit-hungry bosses. Out in the countryside their counterparts were burning hayricks and waylaying the farmers they blamed for high corn prices. There was so much rural unrest

that more soldiers were kept busy at home guarding the property of the wealthy than the Duke of Wellington had under
his command in the war against Napoleon. British society
was in chaos. A single event that symbolised this widespread
malaise was the sight of thousands of people outside Newgate
prison on 18 May. The crowd had come to witness a hanging.
Nothing unusual about that. But, when the condemned man
appeared, he was cheered wildly and onlookers called out
'God bless you!' So popular was the man on the scaffold that
the government had brought 5,000 troops out of barracks to
prevent a potential uprising. Who was this hero of the people
and what had he done? He was a pathetic figure by the name
of John Bellingham and, a week earlier, he had assassinated
the Prime Minister, Spencer Perceval.

Shocking as that event might seem – and it was the first
and last time an elected British executive head was murdered
– even more striking was the reaction, inside and outside
government. Or, rather, the lack of reaction. No national
breast-beating, no state funeral with high-flown oratory. As
one historian put it succinctly, the death of Perceval 'simply
produced yet another ministerial crisis'. That throwaway line
points us in an important direction. If we want to know what
was rotten in 1812 Britain, we have to start at the top.

King George III was blind and mad. His reign had begun
in 1760, and indeed few people could remember a time when
'Farmer George' had not been on the throne. He had once
been a conscientious and largely popular monarch. But by now
mental and physical incapacity had pushed him to the
sidelines of power. In February 1812, the Prince of Wales
was invested with full authority to act as regent. He was a
bird of a very different feather. Fat, indolent, pleasure-

loving and petulant, he had grown up estranged from his father and was the despair of his father's ministers. More than once the Treasury had had to bale him out because of his gambling debts and lavish expenditure. As head of state, 'Prinny' provided neither political nor moral leadership. Since 1796 he had been estranged from his wife, Princess Caroline, who, like a later Princess of Wales, enjoyed the sympathy of most of the population. He had then taken up with a succession of mistresses. There was nothing unusual about that. What annoyed people and fuelled countless indignant sermons was his defiantly exhibitionist behaviour. His principal residences, Carlton House in London and the Royal Pavilion in Brighton, were constantly being extended and refurbished in extravagantly 'un-English' styles and used for ever more elaborate parties. Ordinary people, who were unlikely to read about him in newspapers, clustered instead round the windows of Samuel Fores' shop in Piccadilly and Hannah Humphrey's in St James's, to laugh at the caricatures on display, the obese, sybaritic slob depicted by James Gillray, Isaac Cruikshank and other master satirists.

If, for most Britons, their ruler had become a figure of fun, there were some who could see little humour in a head of state who was ridiculed at home and abroad and who partied while many of his subjects suffered in dire poverty. They vented their indignation by scrawling graffiti on walls offering a hundred guineas for Prinny's head on a plate or by sending him hate mail. 'Bread or Blood!' read one missive addressed to the regent's secretary, 'Tell your master he is a *Damned Unfeeling Scoundrel*'. Their 'betters', of course, had a different take on the antics of the royal court. Aristocrats and social climbers fawned on the Prince Regent and were eager to be counted among his friends, the result being that Prinny set the tone for high society, one which:

> *...swilled and reswilled and repeated their boozings*
> *Till their shirts became dyed with purpureal oozings*

The 50-year-old head of state, who had for several decades waited impatiently for his father to die and pass on the crown, completely blew it when his chance came. As one MP remarked to a friend about the Prince Regent's drinking habits, 'I much doubt whether all the alcohol in the world will be able to brace his nerves up to the mark of facing the difficulties he will soon have to encounter.' It would, in fact, have taken a man of golden character and iron will to stamp his authority on a parliament that was a snakepit of Tory, Whig and Radical rivalries. Over the years the Prince had backed the Whigs, led by Charles James Fox, largely out of spite against his father who supported William Pitt's Tories. But the two big political fish of the age had both died in 1806. They were replaced by minnows.

A nation led by nonentities can muddle along if it is not confronted by serious crises. But Britain in 1812 was engaged in a ruinous war which had been going on for 19 years and showed little sign of coming to a satisfactory end. The egalitarian ideals of the French Revolution had been spread by force to neighbouring countries, threatening to topple all comfortably established monarchies. Britain had, by degrees, emerged as the leader of the old order and there had been some military successes. But, by the dawn of the new century, France had found itself a leader of military and political genius – Napoleon Bonaparte – who soon threatened our island nation with invasion. In 1805, that threat had been disposed of by Nelson and the British navy at Trafalgar. The country had gone wild with patriotic rejoicing; somewhat prematurely. The war had continued. By 1812, Napoleon had pronounced himself emperor of a state which, with its dependent territories, stretched from Gibraltar to the Niemen and from the Baltic to the toe of Italy. The French dictator might have lost control of the seas but he considered that he no longer needed them.

Fat, indolent, pleasure-loving and petulant, the Prince of Wales, 'Prinny', provided neither political nor moral leadership.

As long as he could close Europe to British trade, he could strangle the country he contemptuously regarded as a 'nation of shopkeepers'. By the end of 1811 he seemed to be proved right. The value of British exports had dropped from £60 million to less than £40 million in under a year.

In Westminster, the situation was a mess. The two most able politicians, George Canning and Viscount Castlereagh, refused to serve in the same administration. And, despite the dire national and international situation, the party leaders refused to fuse their interests in a coalition. The Tory majority in the House of Commons was wafer thin and it was only after a great deal of backroom negotiating that, at the end of 1809, a government team had been cobbled together, under the leadership of Spencer Perceval as Prime Minister and Chancellor of the Exchequer. Few observers gave it any chance of surviving more than a few months. The big question it had to face was whether or not to persevere with a war that was crippling the country and growing more unpopular by the month. Militarily there was little to encourage flag-waving. Wellington's forces were inching their way through Portugal and Spain, pushing Napoleon's allies before them but, without the extra men and supplies he was urgently calling for, Wellington was facing a war of attrition.

Could the country afford to drag out the conflict interminably? The trade crisis had provoked raging inflation. All over the country businesses were going bankrupt. To take just one industry as an example, iron and steel production, 9,000 workers were laid off in Birmingham in 1811 and the furnaces of Sheffield were at half capacity. And this despite the fact that the war produced a steady demand for metal. Many of those fortunate enough to stay in work had to endure wage reductions. A weaver earning 13s. 3d. a week in 1800 had seen his income slump to 6s. 4d. by 1812. To make matters worse for every British family, especially the poorer ones, the harvests of 1809 and 1810 had been disastrous. The price of a loaf of bread hit an all time high in 1812. In 1803 it had been 8 d. Now it was 1s. 3d.

Somewhat surprisingly, Perceval managed to hold the government together. He was a man of impeccable virtue, an earnest Evangelical and a passionate patriot. Quite the opposite to the Carlton House crew. Yet, it was his misfortune to find himself just as unpopular as the Prince Regent. The main reason was his unyielding opposition to anything that might undermine the war effort. There were those who believed that the real conflict was not with Napoleon but with the upholders of iniquitous political and judicial systems at home which bore down heavily on the poorer sections of the populace. Radical campaigners, while not supporting the excesses of the French revolutionaries, sympathised with their ideals for a reordering of society. Needless to say, such convictions alarmed the propertied class, who feared that any challenge to the existing order would result in tumbrels trundling down Whitehall and the guillotine set up in Covent Garden. Perceval's uncompromising stance marked him out to many as the enemy of the people.

Londoners also remembered two episodes in 1810 that had cast a black stain over the Prime Minister's reputation. William Cobbett was a radical journalist whose outspoken articles touched a raw nerve among the establishment. The government was determined to silence him. Their chance came when he published a diatribe against some militiamen who had been brutally flogged at Ely. His protest was denounced as seditious. Cobbett was sentenced to two years in Newgate and fined a thumping £1,000. He emerged in 1812, a ruined man. Perceval did not find it so easy to deal with Cobbett's friend, Sir Francis Burdett MP. The popular member for Westminster had made a name for himself by denouncing English prison conditions as worse than those in Paris under the *ancien régime*. He went on to become a real thorn in the flesh to the government. In 1810 they thought they had him. He published a letter in Cobbett's magazine, the *Political Register*, and this was decreed to be a violation of parliamentary privilege. He refused to surrender himself and took refuge in his Piccadilly house. Word spread quickly. Thousands of supporters gathered to prevent officials arresting Burdett, then paraded in the very streets that Nash planned to keep them out of, ordering householders to place lighted candles in their windows as a sign of support. Anyone who refused found himself without windows to light. Then they went on the rampage, singling out the houses of members of the government.

> Wherever there is a minister's house or that of any other un-
> popular man, a flying party of the mob attack it, shatter the
> windows, abuse the inhabitants and break open the door…

So one eye witness recorded after the crisis had passed.
Even then she felt nervous:

> We are far from comfortable now, though the thing is done,
> for the people have threatened all sorts of horrors in revenge
> for their defeat.

What of Burdett? It was only after Guards regiments had
been called out to clear the streets, firing their muskets over
the crowd that the parliamentary Sergeant-at-Arms dared to
go and arrest him. Even then no-one could prevent the MP's
supporters turning out to cheer all along the route through
the City as Burdett was conveyed to the Tower of London.
When the escort left to return to barracks they were set upon
at Tower Hill and in the ensuing fracas several people were
killed. The government went into panic. The Tower was put
in a state of defence, cannon loaded and the dried-out moat
refilled with water. Fifty thousand troops were strategically
stationed around the capital, ready to deal with any uprising among London's *sans culottes*. Burdett was quietly released
after a few weeks.

He did not remain quiet. In 1812 he was re-elected for
Westminster, and went on to form the Hampden Club, the
first of a series of clubs set up to agitate for constitutional reform. Political clubs had been outlawed ever since the French
Revolution had inspired British radicals to press for changes
in the electoral system but Burdett and his colleagues found a

loophole in the law. The Hampden Clubs could not be challenged as organs of a subversive, underground movement, for each was technically independent and autonomous. They could not be accused of inciting mob rule because membership was restricted to men of substance. To all intents and purposes these were respectable and responsible gentlemen's clubs. It was becoming disturbingly clear to Britain's rulers that radicalism was a broad church.

Enter John Bellingham, the joker in the pack. An outsider, an irrelevance almost. He had little or nothing to do with the great issues of the day. He was no campaigner for human rights. When he put a pistol in his pocket and walked from his London lodgings to the parliament house, he had no ideas in his head about widening the suffrage or forcing down the price of corn. John Bellingham was one of life's unfortunates, a 42-year-old businessman who had tried his hand at several careers – and failed in all of them. He had started out as an apprentice to a Whitechapel jeweller but had fallen out with his boss and run away to sea. He must have been something of a Jonah, for his ship ran aground and was wrecked. Next he appeared trading on his own account from a shop in London's Oxford Street. That enterprise lasted less than a year. He was declared bankrupt. Probably he spent some time in a debtors' prison, for he disappears from the records until 1804. By then he was travelling abroad as a commercial agent for various British principals and had reached Archangel, the northernmost Russian port on the White Sea. If he thought that all his problems were thousands of miles behind him, he was mistaken, for he now managed to fall foul of the Russian authorities. Five years in a jail in the semi-frozen north may well have turned his mind (Bellingham's father had died

ROBERT OWEN

Jane Austen was not the only writer who, in 1812, was putting the finishing touches to an important book. Robert Owen, in his Scottish home, was preparing for the publication of a revolutionary pamphlet, *A New View of Society*. Owen (1771-1858) was a self-made man who had amassed a considerable fortune in textiles and was proprietor of the New Lanark Mills, near Glasgow. But he was unlike most industrialists of the new machine age who, in his words, 'have been trained to direct all their faculties to buy cheap and sell dear' without any regard for their workers.

In his factories Owen put into practice his own progressive ideas. His employees (including women and children) worked for ten hours a day, whereas those of his competitors were at their looms throughout all the daylight hours. He provided schools for their children and shops where his workers could buy food at fair prices. During the war of 1812, when mills closed because US cotton suppliers boycotted British ports, most mill owners laid off their workers. Owen continued to employ his on full wages.

Robert Owen was not a full-blown radical like those who wanted to turn society upside down even if it meant (as in France) heads rolling. He was more of a paternalistic philanthropist; he was deeply conscious of the injustice and greed that were the foundations of the existing system. He showed that individuals could challenge the system without resorting to violence. Sadly, his was almost a lone voice.

insane). He developed a persecution complex, fed by resentment at the refusal of the British consul to come to his aid. Back in England in 1809, he married and settled down in Liverpool, now trying his hand as an insurance agent. But his rage at the government's failure to help him during his incarceration had become an obsession. He deserted his wife and children, travelled to London and spent what little money he had left in trying to obtain compensation. When he could find no-one prepared to listen to him, he reasoned (if that is the right word) that the government was the source of all his ills and must be made to pay. Was it not the holier-than-thou Spencer Perceval who was the very personification of an arrogant establishment that cared nothing for the plight of honest working men? On 11 May 1812, John Bellingham, self-proclaimed agent of a higher justice, entered the lobby of the House of Commons and waited for the Prime Minister to emerge from the chamber. When the Premier appeared, his assassin fired one shot at his heart. Perceval died instantly. Bellingham's aim was one of the few things that did not fail him.

This atrocity threw the government into a frenzy. Their immediate reaction was that Bellingham must have been a revolutionary and that his deed was the signal for a general uprising. Even when the truth came out at the assassin's trial, Perceval's colleagues feared that the death of the Prime Minister would be the signal for widespread violent demonstrations. Well might they have been alarmed. Disturbing news soon reached them from all over the country. In Nottingham, jubilant revellers 'paraded the town with drums beating and flags flying'. In Stoke, news of the assassination was brought by a man who 'came running down the street, leaping into the air, waving his hat round his head and shouting with frantic joy, "Perceval is shot, hurrah! Perceval is shot, hurrah!" '

The government rushed Bellingham's case through the court and made sure that his execution took place as soon as possible, before anti-government forces had time to organise. Lord Byron was typically insouciant about Bellingham's death: 'After sitting up all night I saw Bellingham launched into eternity and at three the same day I saw Lady Caroline Lamb launched into the country.' The government could not afford to be so nonchalant. They tried every means possible to put people off attending the execution. Extra barriers were arranged around the scaffold. Posters on walls near Newgate warned, 'Beware of entering the Crowd! Remember Thirty Poor Creatures were pressed to death when Haggerty and Holloway were executed.' The reference was to a tragedy that had occurred five years earlier when a record number of 45,000 had been attracted to the despatching of two notorious murderers. Then, 30 people had, indeed, been crushed to death and a further fourteen badly injured. Clearly, the government feared a similar turnout for Bellingham. Remembering that the presence of troops had, in the Burdett riots two years earlier, incited the mob to erect barricades in Piccadilly, they kept troops at a distance. Cavalry were held in readiness at Lambeth and others were brought into the city limits. The *Times* did its best to play down the event, claiming that heavy rain reduced the size of the crowd and that only a minority cheered the condemned man, but other 'non-establishment' accounts insisted that the watchers had given Bellingham a rousing hero's send-off. The poet Coleridge was heard to mutter, 'This is but the beginning.'

A VOLUPTUARY under the horrors of Digestion.

JAMES GILLRAY'S OBESE, SYBARITIC PRINCE REGENT

The sudden removal of the Prime Minister provoked another round of unseemly squabbling among the leading figures at Westminster. The Prince Regent gave no lead. As soon as he was in power he dumped the Whigs, positive proof that he had little interest in actual policies. He was content to let the party leaders and their accomplices slug it out. Insults were exchanged, bribes offered, deals struck. It was 7 June before a new administration was formed under the leadership of the Earl of Liverpool. It had two main objectives, two national enemies it resolved to pursue with the utmost rigour – Napoleon Bonaparte and the leaders of working-class discontent. The reactionary Tory cabinet draped itself in the union flag and called upon loyal Britons to wage unremitting war against those who threatened the nation from without and within.

Britain by this time was, in fact, two nations; those who were intent on preserving a status quo which served them very well, the self-satisfied landowners and professional people portrayed by Jane Austen, and those who were desperate for social and political change. The dividing line did not run along clear-cut class frontiers. Among the British elite there were many who sympathised with the unemployed and impoverished. Local philanthropists set up relief schemes. Judges – called upon to pronounce sentence on men found guilty of affray, loom-breaking or assault – often erred on the side of leniency. When the government introduced a bill to bring in the death penalty for attacks on factory property, it was Lord Byron who spoke for many when he protested in the House of Lords:

When a proposal is made to emancipate or relieve, you hesitate, you deliberate for years, you temporise and tamper with the minds of men; but a death-bill must be passed off hand, without a thought of the consequences… As the sword is the worst argument that can be used, so should it be the last… The present measure will, indeed, pluck it from the sheath; yet had proper meetings been held in the earlier stages of these riots, had the grievances of these men and their masters (for they also have their grievances) been fairly weighed and justly examined, I do think that means might have been devised to restore these workmen to their avocations, and tranquillity to the country.

He was whistling in the wind. In the early months of 1812 outbreaks of violent protest had become so frequent and widespread that the government could see only increased force as the answer. The new leader, Liverpool, pinned all his hopes on winning the war in Europe and thus restoring commercial prosperity, which alone would provide bread for hungry stomachs. Unfortunately, ruined businessmen and unemployed artisans could not wait for the dawning of that happy day. And so King Ludd established his brief and turbulent reign.

This mythical monarch had first raised his standard at the end of 1811 in Nottingham, where gangs of hosiers, seeing their livelihoods threatened by the new looms, went on an orgy of machine-smashing. Like a rain-starved forest, the industrial Midlands and the north were only waiting for this spark to burst into flame. Within weeks of the hosiers' rampage, workers in other textile industries were emulating their Nottinghamshire brothers. Masked gangs gathered at night to carry out their work of destruction and there was little the authorities could do to stop them. No-one knew where the Luddites would strike next. By the time a mill owner had gathered a band of servants or sent for the militia, the attackers had dissolved into the darkness. Sometimes they issued warnings:

> In justice to humanity We think it our Bounin Duty to give you this Notice that is if you do Not Cause those Dressing Machines to be Remov'd Within the Bounds of Seven Days… your factory and all that it Contains will and shall Surely Be Set on Fire…

Before the end of the winter Luddism had become a movement, with its own organisation, rules, champions and martyrs. From underground presses came broadsheets and ballads:

> *You Heroes of England who wish to have a trade*
> *Be true to each other and be not afraid.*
> *Tho' bayonet is fixed they can do no good*
> *As long as we keep up the Rules of General Ludd.*

There was much truth in the assertion that the militia was powerless against them. Not only were the ringleaders difficult to track down; many of the common soldiery were sympathetic to the lawbreakers. Magistrates, manufacturers and landowners were frustrated at their inability to bring the Luddite rabble under control.

It could not be long before blood was spilled. The gangs broke into houses and armed themselves with stolen muskets and pistols. The factory owners distributed weapons to their servants. They organised night shifts to defend their properties. In April 1812, when 150 Luddites raided Rawfolds

Mill in Yorkshire, they were driven off and left behind several wounded and two dead comrades. George Mellor of Huddersfield, a leading Luddite activist, decided to avenge his fallen friends. The man he marked out for destruction was William Horsfall of Ottiwells, near Huddersfield. This choleric mill owner had turned his premises into a fortress defended by soldiers and cannons, making no secret of his contempt for the enemy. 'Let them come to Ottiwells,' he taunted, 'and I'll ride up to my saddle girth in Luddite blood.' On 27 April, Mellor and three accomplices laid in wait for Horsfall on the route he took every day to his factory. And they gunned him down. It was a turning point. That single act brought the prospect of French-style revolution terrifyingly close. From now on the struggle was no longer just about the introduction of machines. Different streams of discontent merged. In Manchester a group of women attacked farmers who were selling potatoes at high prices. Food riots were widespread. A Luddite manifesto issued in May declared:

> It is the opinion of our general and men that as long as that blackguard drunken whoring fellow called Prince Regent and his servants have anything to do with government that nothing but distress will befall us.

The propertied classes subsequently closed ranks, demanding tough government action. Britain teetered on the brink of class war.

Liverpool and his Home Secretary, Viscount Sidmouth, would have loved to have at their disposal surveillance cameras, ID cards and DNA testing. They had to make do with more traditional control and detection methods – paid informers, interrogation under torture, agents provocateurs

WHEREAS,

Several EVIL-MINDED PERSONS have assembled together in a riotous Manner, and DESTROYED a NUMBER of

FRAMES,

In different Parts of the Country:

THIS IS

TO GIVE NOTICE,

That any Person who will give Information of any Person or Persons thus wickedly

BREAKING THE FRAMES,

Shall, upon CONVICTION, receive

50 GUINEAS

REWARD.

And any Person who was actively engaged in RIOTING, who will impeach his Accomplices, shall, upon CONVICTION, receive the same Reward, and every Effort made to procure his Pardon.

☞ Information to be given to Messrs. COLDHAM and ENFIELD.

Nottingham, March 26, 1811.

'THE PROPERTIED CLASSES EVENTUALLY CLOSED RANKS AGAINST THE LUDDITES, DEMANDING TOUGH GOVERNMENT ACTION...'.

and spies. But these proved effective enough. In May, four offenders were hanged for setting fire to a Westhoughton mill. One of them was a boy of twelve. According to a local journalist the real villain of the piece was the magistrate, Colonel Fletcher, whose agents provocateurs had incited the mob. Magistrates and circuit judges who had proved themselves too lenient were replaced with harsher, merciless ones. With the appointment of the likes of the uncompromising Sir Simon Le Blanc, hangings and transportations rapidly increased. Luddite raids continued well into the autumn until, finally, the forces of law and order prevailed. In October, after a prolonged and determined investigation, Mellor and his aids were tracked down and arrested. Le Blanc presided over their state trial in January 1813. As a result seventeen Luddites were executed.

By this time the government had yet more worries. On 19 August HMS. *Guerrière* was captured after a two and half hour engagement with the American warship *Constitution*. Two months later the USS sloop *Wasp* made even shorter work of HMS. *Frolic*. These proud British ships belonged to the world's greatest navy, Nelson's navy, the navy that reputedly ruled the waves! The effect on morale was catastrophic. It was the final blow to an already reeling country. But why were British and American vessels battering each other on the high seas? Because Britain, almost a generation after the granting of independence, found itself once more at war with her ex-colonists. US President James Madison had made the fateful declaration on 18 June.

The two governments blundered into hostilities as a result of stupidity, hubris and stubbornness. Oh, and a slice of sheer bad luck. On one side was a country at a desperately low ebb, fighting a military and economic war with France. On the other, a new nation desperately trying to establish itself on equal terms with the states of Europe and, therefore, sensitive to any slight which appeared to be made against it. One British priority was keeping up the strength of the navy. It had established the right to search any foreign ship and press-gang any British sailors who might be found. American captains resented having their vessels boarded, especially when crew members claiming American citizenship were hauled off to fight for the old enemy. Back on shore, the boundary line between Canada and the USA was also a source of friction. Settlers south of the line were engaged in the ongoing bullying and butchering of the native American Indians and the seizure of their grazing and hunting grounds. They believed – with some justification – that the 'savages' often received succour and aid from the British territory across the border.

But the main American complaint was against trade discrimination. France and Britain were waging economic as well as military war against each other. As part of this they tried to prevent other nations from trading with the enemy. This affected American merchants badly. In 1810 Napoleon hit on a diplomatic ploy; he offered to lift his ban on US shipping – if Britain would do the same. His object was to create a dilemma for his foes. If the British government followed suit, France would benefit from the lifting of the commercial embargo. If they did not, they would provoke resentment among their ex-colonists. Many politicians in Washington clearly saw the French move for what it was. But President Madison fell for it. He demanded Britain's compliance and backed this up by closing American ports to British ships. This was potentially ruinous to the merchants of both countries and Madison received loud protests from New England politicians and trading communities. But he was deaf to their complaints.

The President's stubbornness played well with the hawks in his own administration, with frontiersmen who had their own reasons for anti-British sentiment and with rednecks who harboured resentment against the old enemy. Prejudice was just as strong on the other side of the Atlantic. A geographical treatise published in 1809 confidently assured its readers:

> The common people of the United States in general show what they call their independent spirit by surliness of behaviour, and a contempt of those trifling civilities which distinguish men accustomed to decent life from those who are reared in barbarism.

The tragedy was that the British government was actually-well disposed to responding to Madison's demand and lifting trade restrictions. By February 1812, Spencer Perceval had decided to rescind the orders in council against neutral shipping but Bellingham's bullet had put a stop to that. The confusion and reorganisation following the Prime Minister's death further delayed discussion of the American problem and it was only on 16 June that Lord Castlereagh, the Foreign Secretary, announced the immediate lifting of the trade ban. This news had not reached Washington by 18 June, when Madison declared war. Britain and America thus found themselves involved in the wrong war for the wrong reasons against the wishes of large sections of their own people.

By the end of the year, Britain had had to divert from the European theatre troops it could ill afford to lose. It had suffered humiliation at sea at the hands of a navy dismissed by our last-quoted author as 'contemptible'. And it was having to fend off invasions of Canada. And this was by no means a remote war with little impact at home. As well as the unwanted commitment of men, money and material to the conflict, and the further disruption of inter-continental trade, it involved settlers on both sides of the border, settlers who had anxious relatives in the old country.

When, in Jane Austen's *Sense and Sensibility*, Lady Middleton 'exerted herself to ask Mr. Palmer if there was any news in the paper', he replied "No, none at all", – and read on'. Well-bred ladies were not expected to trouble themselves with national and international affairs. Perhaps, in 1812, it was as well. Ignorance of the true state of the nation may have saved them from a great deal of grief.

AFTERWORD

You may protest that 1812 was also the year of Napoleon's calamitous retreat from Moscow, and therefore quite a good year for Britain. Well, yes and no. Certainly, the Russian campaign was an unmitigated disaster for France. By the time the Emperor struggled back through the early Russian and Polish winter in November, his Grande Armée of 453,000 men had been decimated – with only 10,000 left fit for combat. At the end of 1812, France's enemies could indeed detect a glimmer of light at the end of the tunnel. But it was only a glimmer. Napoleon Bonaparte was by no means finished. It would be another two and a half years before he was finally defeated at Waterloo and, even then, as Wellington himself admitted, it was 'a damned nice thing – the nearest run thing you ever saw in your life'.

What Happened Before...

1929	Wall Street Crash sparked Great Depression.
	Labour government formed by Ramsay Macdonald
1931	Hitler becomes German Chancellor with dictatorial powers.
	Japan left League of Nations.
1934	Churchill warned of growing German air menace.
	Launch of S.S. *Queen Mary*
1935	Baldwin formed national government.
	Germany rejected Versailles Treaty

1936-7   ROTTENEST YEAR

...And What Came After

1938	Chamberlain made Munich Agreement with Hitler.
	Germany occupied Czech Sudetenland.
	Launch of S.S. *Queen Elizabeth*
1939	Virtual collapse of League of Nations.
	Hitler invaded Poland.
	Britain and France declared war.

1936-7

I KNOW IT is a terribly unpopular thing to say but I find our annual Remembrance Day activities depressing. Not because of the recollection of the sacrifice members of our armed forces have made in various wars. I am all in favour of taking time out to focus on the bravery and heroism which go some way towards redeeming the folly of war. Certainly not because I resent the Poppy Day appeal. As a historian I know that for centuries we have cruelly neglected the men and women we send to fight our battles for us.

No, what it is that sticks in my throat is the year-on-year repetition of those early newsreels of 1914-18 trench warfare (some of which were faked by the government of the day) and the constant harping on about the campaign on the western front, as though it was the only (or, at least, the worst) example of appalling carnage in the whole history of warfare. Some would argue that it is precisely this highlighting of muddy, bloody horror that concentrates our minds on the awfulness of war. My response to that is that if the sheer obscenity of this shameful campaign really had shocked world governments into ensuring that the 1914-18 holocaust would be the war to end all wars, then there would be something worth celebrating about it. We all know it did not. All the sacrifices of that ghastly confrontation of national hatreds were, from the historical viewpoint, made in vain. So far from solving any of the problems facing the nations, World War I simply accelerated the slide towards the abyss of an even worse war and the development of weapons of truly appalling destructive potential. Every human tragedy, whether individual or national, is wretched, but it is rendered worse if there is nothing we can, or do, learn from it.

So, despite the undoubted horrors of the 'Kaiser's War', I don't intend to single out any part of that event as a rottenest year. Apart from anything else, total war does tend to have a positive effect on those caught up in it. It unites people as nothing else can. The spirit of nationalism is stirred. Everyone has a common objective. In 1915 all that mattered to the British people was defeating Germany. After victory had been achieved, Britain basked for a long time in the euphoric glow of victory. People mourned their dead but believed that their sacrifice had not been in vain; that British values and principles had been vindicated. It took a while for the chilling realisation to come home to people that the war had solved nothing. *That* was when depression set in. We need to identify the turning point and I believe that 1936-7 stands out as the pivotal time. The barometer of national confidence which, after a period of 'Change', had pointed to 'Set Fair' now slipped steadily and ominously towards 'Stormy'. It dawned, at least on the more perceptive of British men and women, that the victory of 1918 had been no more than a temporary cessation of hostilities.

Britain, like all the other countries of the Western world, had had a very bumpy ride since the end of the First World War. Governments rose and fell. Expectations were high throughout these years. After any war the natural desire of the winners is to get back to 'the way things were'. There is a reluctance to believe that fundamental issues remain unresolved or that the war has actually created new problems. What the peacemakers at Versailles were intent on achieving in 1919 was international security and a return to 'normality'. To ensure the former, the League of Nations was called into being, a body which would, supposedly, curb the ambitions of potential aggressors and provide a forum for the peaceful settlement of disputes. Germany was disarmed and the major powers put in place measures designed to prevent the kind of arms race that had accelerated the march to war in the early years of the century. By 'normality' what the industrialised nations basically meant was the resumption of international trade patterns that would guarantee them markets for their manufactured goods and, therefore, their prosperity.

For a time it seemed that these objectives might be realised. There was a post-war boom and at least the appearance of political stability in most of the countries that had been involved in the recent conflict. But the old world dominated by kings, emperors and their courts had gone. The Tsar of Russia, the Austrian Emperor and the Kaiser of the German Empire were no more and everywhere the very concept of monarchical government was challenged. The overthrow of old tyrannies had unleashed new aspirations and no country was exempt from their influence. Some idealists admired Soviet Bolshevism and saw it as the trail-blazer of the political future. Others viewed with alarm the prospect of proletarian revolution and looked to the fascist regimes emerging in Germany and Italy for the kind of strong government they believed essential for any well-ordered state.

Where was liberal democracy in all this? Sadly, the 'victor' nations lacked the energy to steer Europe towards permanent peace and stability. With the exception of the USA, they had fought themselves to exhaustion and had had to expend most of their energies on national recovery. They demonstrated little ability, and, in some cases, little will to put the past behind and concentrate on the construction of a new and better world. The xenophobia roused by the war was not dissipated by the peace treaties which ended it. Old hatreds lingered, summarised by the words of one British politician, who vowed to squeeze Germany 'till you can hear the pips squeak'. New central European states had been carved out of the old empires, adding thousands of kilometres of new frontiers which were bound to cause fresh arguments. But the League of Nations lacked the military 'teeth' to do much about these disputes. Mainly because it did not include the Americans. America was emerging as the world's economic leader but, after intervening in the late war, its citizens were determined not to become entangled again in the crises of Europe. They could and did provide financial aid for the rebuilding of shattered economies but any assistance was supplied at arm's length.

Could Britain not have exerted itself more forcefully? After all, it had, for the greater part of a century, been policing its own world-spanning empire. The truth is that the suffering of 1914-18 and the economic and social dislocation resulting from the war had left the nation punch-drunk. The old two-party system in which Liberals and Conservatives vied for power had disappeared with the emergence of the Labour Party. In the politics of the 1920s, the only certainty was uncertainty. Between 1919 and 1931 there were eight changes of government. In one two-year period alone (November 1922 to October 1924) there were three general elections. None of the solutions offered by conventional politicians seemed to have any real impact on people's lives, so it is hardly surprising that significant numbers of British people began looking to the more extreme politics of continental Europe for answers – Communism, the rule of the proletariat, and Fascism, right-wing dictatorship.

Soon, however, Britain had worse problems to worry about than finding the right political ideology. In October 1929, with the Wall Street Crash, the world was plunged into recession – the Great Depression. Over-confidence in America's economic strength pushed share prices to absurd levels. When investors rushed to cash in at the top of the market, share values plummeted, banks collapsed, companies went out of business and unemployment soared. The international knock-on effect was immediate. Countries, particularly Germany – which was impoverished by the financial punishments imposed by the victors of 1918 – saw

> Churchill, that great sculptor of speeches, castigated the government for being 'decided only to be undecided, resolved to be irresolute, adamant for drift, solid for fluidity, all-powerful to be impotent.

the value of their currencies collapse and were sucked into a financial maelstrom.

When a similar international economic crisis occurred in 2008, many commentators looked back to the Great Depression for parallels. Comparisons can certainly be made but in one key respect the world of 80 years ago was a very different place. The basic tragedy of the 1920s and 1930s was that countries had no idea of how to act together in times of peace.

Internationalism was in its very infancy. Diplomacy was still directed towards achieving political 'balance' by signing treaties. Thus, France strengthened its ties with the Soviet Union in 1936 in order to counteract the power of Germany. At the same time Britain reached an agreement on naval building with Germany in order to safeguard its long distance imperial supply lines. Both sets of negotiations were carried out in secret. Both had the effect of straining relations between the old allies. And nations that were incapable of developing a joint vision for worldwide peace were hardly likely to be able to act in concert for the restoration of economic stability. Each state was preoccupied in protecting its own commercial infrastructure. And so at the very time that governments should have been encouraging cross-border trade they were erecting tariff walls to prevent cheap imports damaging their home industries.

But the bad times did pass – or so it seemed. By 1931 the world's economic leaders were slowly beginning to climb out of the trough. People persuaded themselves that things could only get better. In 1935 Britain's Chancellor of the Exchequer, Neville Chamberlain, proudly announced, 'Broadly speaking, we may say that we have recovered in this country

by 80 per cent of our prosperity'. Like most political pro-
nouncements, this one involved a certain amount of massag-
ing of statistics. Recovery was by no means evenly spread.
There were areas of Britain's industrial heartland where the
majority of men were still out of work and Chamberlain had
set up a new Assistance Board to distribute relief to the worst-
affected families. But unemployment had fallen steadily from
its 1932 peak of 2.7 million to below 2 million and was still
dropping. Industrial output was up and the cost of living had
fallen an impressive thirteen per cent since the black days of
the Great Depression. Political life had achieved some stability. Since 1931 the country had been run by a national government which, by incorporating members from both major
parties, demonstrated unity and the determination to put
aside policy differences in the interests of recovery. In May
1935 Britain cheered itself with enthusiastic celebrations of
King George V's silver jubilee. There were still many people
around who could remember the last royal holiday of 1897,
when the country had been *en fête* in honour of Queen Vic-
toria's 60-year reign. Perhaps the 'good old days' really were
returning.

The new year began ominously. King George V died,
after a short illness, on 20 January. His people mourned the
passing of a monarch who had headed the country with dignity and sober patriotism through years of great crisis. There
was, however, a bright side to the situation: it brought to the
throne the popular, raffish, 41-year-old Prince Edward, who
promised to be a breath of fresh air. He was an extrovert
socialite with a distinct dislike of his father's favourite 'fuddy-
duddy' ministers. Chief among these was Stanley Baldwin,
for whom 1936 became an *annus horribilis*. He had been con-

firmed in office as prime minister at the general election of
the previous November, but public confidence in him had
come under attack because of his weak handling of foreign
affairs. Baldwin was, above all else, an astute party politician. His answer to the confusion of the 1920s was to build
up a strong Conservative Party. In all his decisions he kept a
wary eye on their electoral consequences. What was likely to
prove popular he trumpeted; acts likely to provoke criticism
he did his best to keep secret. He was an experienced public
performer. He carried an aura of upper-class authority and
was an effective speaker both in the Commons and on the
hustings. This meant that he was usually able to sway debate
in favour of his own policies, however dubious. It was Britain's great misfortune to have such a man at the helm in such
crisis times.

The basic problem was the worsening international
situation. The British people, almost to a man and woman,
were determined to maintain peace, but their political and
diplomatic leaders knew how difficult that was becoming
and were divided on the best way to deal with the situation.
A new breed of dictators had emerged around the world
who were contemptuous of what the victors of 1918 held
sacred. Adolf Hitler and his National Socialist (Nazi) government were rearming Germany, in repudiation of the
Versailles Treaty. Belligerent regimes in Italy and Japan
had successfully defied the League of Nations, which had
proved to have no effective means of enforcing its decisions.
It had failed to prevent Japan expanding into Manchuria in
1931 and faced another test in 1935-6 when Italy annexed
Abyssinia. Baldwin tried secretly to sponsor a compromise
deal with the Italian dictator, Benito Mussolini (the Hoare-

Laval Plan). Unfortunately for him, the press got hold of the details. There was a public outcry. All sections of British opinion were affronted by the prospect of a small African state being bullied by a leading European nation. Perceptions had changed totally since the 'Scramble for Africa' of the 1880s, when most Britons had been proud of their country's imperial expansion. Now the press demanded that the League of Nations should take a tough line with Italy. Overnight Baldwin became the nation's public enemy number one.

Early in 1936 Spain provided another cause for concern. The republic was torn between right- and left-wing elements. Tensions grew during the year and came to a head in July, when an army mutiny, led by the fascist, General Franco, seized part of the country and provoked a civil war. For committed European idealists of the left and right this conflict became a test case. Germany, Italy and Russia sent material aid to the warring parties. In Britain intellectuals and journalists agitated for action and some 2,000 young socialists went off to fight beside their Spanish 'brothers'. Before long, the Spanish conflict was polarising political opinion in Britain as a whole. Many of the rising generation of British men and women were moved by the oratory and pamphleteering of extremist agitators. Oswald Mosley, a former Labour MP, founded the British Union of Fascists. In direct emulation of Hitler's semi-military organisations, Mosley's blackshirts held rallies, marched provocatively through Jewish neighbourhoods and distributed literature warning against the 'red menace'.

1936 was the year Britain began, almost surreptitiously, to abandon the policy of disarmament. The country at large might have been set on preserving peace and doing nothing to provoke hostile reaction from the belligerent dictatorships of Europe, but the service chiefs of staff and a minority of politicians were clamouring for the nation to be put into a state of readiness for war. In the run-up to the 1935 election Baldwin had downplayed the 'scaremongering' of those who were calling for Britain to respond more vigorously to German rearmament. Months later, he defended his duplicity in a speech of which Winston Churchill wrote, 'I have never heard such a squalid confession from a public man.' What Baldwin told the House was:

> You will remember at that time there was probably a stronger pacifist feeling running through the country than at any time since the war… My position as leader of a great party was not altogether a comfortable one. I asked myself what chance was there… within the next year or two of that feeling being so changed that the country would give a mandate for rearmament. Supposing I had gone to the country and said that Germany was rearming and we must rearm. Does anybody think that this pacific democracy would have rallied to that cry at that moment? I cannot think of anything that would have made the loss of the election from my point of view more certain.

Development of military equipment had, in fact, not been curtailed after 1918 and the possibilities of aerial warfare, in particular, had intrigued engineers. When, in March 1936, the prototype of R. J. Mitchell's revolutionary Spitfire fighter plane took place, the RAF were so impressed with it that they immediately ordered 310. Mitchell was working on designs for a new, four-engined bomber when he died of cancer the following year at the age of 42. Meanwhile, a no-less impressive innovation was already under way. The *Ark Royal* aircraft carrier, to be launched the following April, ushered in a new era of naval warfare. Another development destined to prove vital to Britain was radar, which had been perfected in 1935 and was by now being installed at stations along the eastern seaboard.

Welcome as such innovations were, the pace of production did not satisfy men like Winston Churchill, who watched Germany's rapid rearmament programme with growing alarm. Churchill, the great sculptor of speeches, castigated the government for being 'decided only to be undecided, resolved to be irresolute, adamant for drift, solid for fluidity, all-powerful to be impotent. So we go on,' he continued, 'preparing more months and years – precious, perhaps vital to the greatness of Britain – for the locusts to eat.' He was the spokesman for that group who were convinced that another war was on the horizon but no-one wanted to listen to such prophets of doom. In the end, the government compromised: defence budgets were increased, inevitably at the cost of other items of government expenditure, but reluctantly and not at a pace likely to deter a potential aggressor. In 1937 Britain would spend less than five per cent of its income on defence. The figures for Germany, Italy, the USSR and Japan were 23.5%, 14.5%, 26.4% and 28.2% respectively. More fundamentally, the political squabbles over rearmament contributed to a mood of growing apprehension in the country. The news from abroad was not reassuring. In November 1936, Germany and Italy announced their solidarity by creating the Berlin-Rome Axis and Germany formed a pact with Japan aimed at checking the advance of international socialism. The right-wing dictatorships had a common purpose and were forging a unity that completely eluded the democratic western powers.

But it was domestic issues which dominated the British headlines. Throughout October 1936, attention was focussed on the Jarrow Crusade. On the 5th, 200 marchers set out from the Tyneside shipbuilding town carrying a petition signed by 11,000 local people. What they were asking for was government assistance in setting up a steel works to replace the heavy industries in their town which had been closed down. This was not the first demonstration aimed at drawing attention to the plight of Britain's unemployment blackspots. The government were well aware of the sufferings being felt in such places as Jarrow, where 68 per cent of the adult male population was out of work. But there were no Tory votes to be won in the industrial northeast so Baldwin merely dismissed the protests and demonstrations as socially divisive, a perilous step along the road to Soviet-style Communism. When Ellen Wilkinson, Labour MP for Jarrow, rose in the House to plead her constituents' cause, she had to suffer Conservative scorn. Her parliamentary opponents dubbed her 'Red Ellen'. The smears worked all too well. Large sections of the British population were nervous of working-class protests and regarded them as subversive. Even Labour parliamentarians boycotted the Jarrow Crusade for fear of the taint of extremism. To avoid any opprobrium being attached to the march, the borough council funded it, declined sponsorship from the National Unemployed Workers' Movement and obtained the blessing of the local church.

But not all the British people were indifferent to the plight of the unemployed. The march became something of a triumphal procession. Led by a band, the crusaders travelled in 22 easy stages the 451 kilometres to London. All along the route they were met by cheering crowds and were provided with food and hospitality. But it all ended in anticlimax. When the marchers reached their destination, Stanley Baldwin simply refused to meet them. They returned empty handed to the place Ellen Wilkinson later called, 'the town that was murdered'.

When Baldwin sent word to the men from Jarrow that he was too busy to see them, there was a shred of truth behind his excuse. The Prime Minister was preoccupied with a very tricky constitutional problem. The new King had been involved for a couple of years in a relationship with an American divorcée, Wallis Simpson. This celebrated love affair divided the nation. Edward had become popular because of his leadership of the smart set, his outspoken opposition to the old King's cool detachment and his visits to poor areas of the country. To those who knew the couple, it was clear that Edward was besotted with his mistress, even though he was not alone in enjoying her favours. His supporters believed that, in a modern, progressive nation, the head of state should be able to choose his own wife. One member of the fashionable set recorded of Mrs Simpson in his diary:

> She is a woman of charm, sense, balance and great wit, with dignity and taste. She has always been an excellent influence on the King, who has loved her openly and honestly. I really consider that she would have been an excellent Queen.

Against such friends were marshalled the forces of reaction, whose attitudes ranged from simple snobbery to Christian conviction. The Church of England opposed divorce and Mrs Simpson was doubly obnoxious because she was in the process of disentangling herself from her *second* husband. The gossips were not slow in getting to work. It was suggested that Wallis was a social-climbing American *femme fatale* who had set her sights on becoming queen. There were even suggestions that she was *very friendly* with Hitler's ambassador and was passing confidential information to him. Edward himself had considerable sympathy with Germany and he did not improve his own position when he delivered a speech urging rapprochement – to the British Legion of all organisations. All this was an embarrassment to the government. They tried to censor the coverage given to the 'Simpson scandal' by the British press but they were powerless to prevent foreign newspapers and journals relishing the scandal.

Nor was Baldwin entirely innocent of personal bias in this sensitive situation. He harboured deep-seated and long-festered antagonism towards Edward. In the clash of cultures between George V and his son, Baldwin had sided unequivocally with the King.. He had disapproved of the Prince's hedonistic lifestyle and had come to doubt his suitability as heir to the throne. Like George V, Baldwin looked towards the continent where thirteen royal dynasties had come to an end since 1914. He believed that the British monarchy could only survive by retaining its traditional dignity and reserve. He was particularly resentful of Edward's love of all things American. The USA was an essential ally but the two countries eyed one another with distinct caution. To many on the other side of the Atlantic, Britain was an insufferably

THE MARCH BECAME SOMETHING OF A TRIUMPHAL PROCESSION. ALL ALONG THE ROUTE THE MEN WERE MET BY CHEERING CROWDS AND WERE PROVIDED WITH FOOD AND HOSPITALITY. (© GETTY IMAGES)

condescending imperialistic power living in the past, while British traditionalists were suspicious of the glamorous and wealthy lifestyle projected through that wonder of the age, the 'talkies'. Baldwin saw the new King as nothing less than a political threat. In a limited monarchy rulers are supposed to bow to the judgement of their prime minister but Edward showed him little respect. Indeed, he regarded it as part of his responsibility to make the monarchy more open and accessible and this involved shaking off the shackles imposed by political dinosaurs like Baldwin.

Throughout most of 1936 there was no constitutional issue at stake. Baldwin might have regarded the royal circle as quite inappropriate but he was powerless to detach Edward from his friends and his mistress. Some members of the court were convinced that the Prime Minister was plotting to remove Edward in favour of his more amenable and pliable brother, Albert, Duke of York and Baldwin's secretive manner certainly encouraged such suspicions. He kept his ministerial colleagues in the dark about his dealings with the palace and whatever 'arrangements' he was making with the press and the Church.

By October Mrs Simpson's divorce proceedings were almost complete and Edward informed the Prime Minister of his intention to marry her as soon as the decree came through. By the time the Jarrow marchers were on their way south, Baldwin was embroiled in the 'Simpson affair'. The press would not be denied. As always thriving on scandal, the national papers were leading the pro and anti factions into battle. The *Mail*, *Express* and *Mirror* were for the King. The *Times* and *Telegraph* campaigned against him. Baldwin, with most of the establishment behind him, pointed out to Edward the unpalatable truth that to marry a divorced woman would be incompatible with his position as head of the English Church. He suggested that the move would be widely unpopular – on both sides of the Atlantic. There were certainly moral issues at stake but the battle was essentially one of tactics – and Baldwin was a seasoned tactician. Edward wanted an open debate so that his supporters could argue his case and muster public support. Baldwin was determined to settle the matter in camera. He refused permission for Edward to deliver a radio message to the people, explaining his situation. When the King asked whether the country would accept a morganatic marriage, whereby Wallis might become his consort but not the nation's queen, Baldwin said he would think about it. However, when he reported to parliament, Baldwin made no mention of the morganatic option. Nor did he utter the word 'abdication' to the Commons. He refused to allow a parliamentary debate. So the negotiations that went on for weeks were discreet to the point of being surreptitious. At the end of October Mrs Simpson's divorce came through.

'This is the end of an age.' So commented Winston Churchill on 30 November 1936. He was referring not to the King's romantic entanglement (he was, in fact, one of Edward's few political supporters) but to a vivid glow he saw in the Kentish sky on his way home from Westminster. The Crystal Palace was on fire. This remarkable and striking piece of Victorian engineering had been built 85 years before as the setting for the Great Exhibition of 1851. At that time Britain had been the world's most technologically advanced country and the hub of international commerce. During the six months of the exhibition, hundreds of thousands of visitors from scores of countries had thronged to admire the exhibits in the glittering cathedral of human ingenuity situated in London's Hyde Park. Subsequently the building had been moved to Penge Common, south of the capital, and been used for a variety of purposes. It had enjoyed a warm place in people's hearts, so much so that when, before World War I, it fell into disrepair and was sold off, a public subscription was raised to reacquire it for the nation. During the war it had been renamed HMS *Victory VI* and used as a naval training centre and later it housed the Imperial War Museum. Its sudden and complete destruction in 1936 thus came as a terrible shock. It was one of those events, insignificant in itself, which makes an enormous impact on public morale. The Crystal Palace had stood as a symbol of British achievement, a visual reminder of the good times. Churchill's verdict was not an exaggeration.

By now King Edward had accepted that he could not have the crown *and* Wallis. His decision was blazoned to the world in press headlines on 1 December: KING TO MARRY 'WALLY' – WEDDING NEXT JUNE. On 10 December Edward signed the abdication agreement renouncing the throne for himself and his heirs for ever. The following day he informed the nation of his decision in a broadcast message. 'I cannot discharge the duties of king as I would wish to do,' he told the millions of listeners gathered around their wireless sets, 'without the help and support of the woman I love.' Now there were – rather belated – demonstrations of support for the ex-King. Marchers paraded outside Buckingham Palace, the Houses of Parliament and 10 Downing Street, demanding Edward's reinstatement. Voices were raised on his behalf in parliament. The powerful press barons, Beaverbrook and Rothermere, campaigned vigorously and tried to form a 'King's party'. Fascist and communist groups linked forces in backing this movement. The banners waved by the demonstrators carried such legends as 'GOD SAVE THE KING – FROM BALDWIN' and, more directly, 'FLOG BALD-

WIN – WE WANT EDWARD'. But the protestors were in a minority. Thanks to Baldwin's cunning handling of the business, we shall never know how a properly informed public might have reacted. Certainly, there were many British people who felt that they had suffered a body blow to their national pride. They believed, not unreasonably, that they had been weighed in the balance against a woman of dubious character – and been found wanting.

Britain entered 1937 in sombre mood. It would be no exaggeration to say that the nation was suffering an identity crisis. According to the *Times'* report of the death of George V a year earlier, the King's last words had been 'How is the empire?' It was an anxiety many people might have shared. In the First World War units from Britain's far-flung colonies and dominions had fought beside soldiers from the mother country with whose interests they associated themselves. Their emotional ties remained strong but, with the passing of the years, they were developing their own regional concerns. Australia was acutely aware of Japanese ambitions. Canada increasingly shared the economic problems and political attitudes of its southern neighbour. By 1937 the 'white' dominions had become 'autonomous nations of an imperial commonwealth'. As the Statute of Westminster (1931) had enunciated, these territories were not subject to the enactments of the imperial government, 'except at the request and with the consent' of their own legislatures. Their progress towards self-determination was steady and inevitable.

India, however, was another matter. Once the jewel in the imperial crown, it had been torn by years of demonstrations and bloody conflict. Eventually this had resulted in a new constitution. In elections held at the end of 1936 the Indian National Congress won a majority of the votes and their goal was the rapid achievement of complete independence. In the complex twentieth-century world, Britain could no longer police her overseas possessions, even had she wanted to. The erstwhile great imperial power was under-resourced and over-extended. This created diplomatic dilemmas. For example, it was obviously desirable to drive a wedge between Germany and Japan, but to reach a better understanding with the oriental power would be to risk damaging relations with Australia – not to mention the USA – while cosying up to Germany would cause friction with France and undermine Britain's precarious leadership role in Europe. People who thought about such things – including politicians – were confused about the nation's position in the new, troubled and bewildering world that was emerging in the late 1930s.

By 1937, everyone knew that Britain and Germany were involved in an arms race. The Chancellor, Neville Chamberlain, announced extra expenditure to be financed by increased government borrowing. Within months, war material was pouring off the assembly lines. Ominously, it included gas masks. The government's military advisers warned that the 'unspeakable Hun', who had employed mustard gas in the trench warfare of 1914-18, would not hesitate to use air power to poison civilian populations. Some people continued to oppose rearmament in principle. They believed that the very fact of preparing for war made war almost inevitable. Others reluctantly supported the new policy in the belief that parity of armaments would be an effective deterrent to aggression. And there were those who accepted stoically that there was going to be a war and were determined to win it. Whatever people's convictions, no-one could be in doubt about the potential menace presented by the Nazi regime. Even if they chose to ignore descriptions of concentration camps and outrages against Jews brought back by travellers in Germany, they had only to watch newsreels of the mass rallies of fanatical supporters at Nuremberg or to hear snatches of the Führer's demagogic oratory to realise that Germany was nursing a culture that must, inevitably, clash withWestern-style democracy.

As 1937 progressed it became clear that the economy was now almost on a war footing. The government had not given up on diplomacy. And the nation had not quite yet abandoned the hope that diplomacy might work. But international negotiations would not be handled by the men who had led Britain for the past fourteen years. Prince Albert had become king as George VI and, after his coronation in May 1937, the Labour leader, Ramsay Macdonald, and Stanley Baldwin went into retirement. Whatever their failings, both leaders had been men of stature. Those who replaced them were politicians of the second or third rank. It was Neville Chamberlain who, in May, stepped up to the plate as Prime Minister. Chamberlain's name will always be associated with appeasement. The popular verdict on him is that he was a weak man, bullied and bamboozled by Hitler. But we would do well to take on board what Baldwin said to him some months later:

> If you can secure peace, you may be cursed by a lot of hotheads but, my word, you will be blessed in Europe and by future generations.

And Germany was very far from being his only problem. Troubling news arrived from all over the world. As recently as April, British public opinion had been stunned to read about Guernica, a Basque fishing village whose civilian population had been bombed by General Franco's German allies. On the other side of the world the Sino-Japanese War was going badly. Japan occupied Peking, Tiensin and Shanghai. The whole world seemed to have gone security crazy. Protective alliances were being struck from Baghdad to Belgrade. Bulgaria signed a non-aggression pact with Yugoslavia; Italy signed with Yugoslavia; and Afghanistan, Iran, Iraq and Turkey followed suit. Those whose memories reached back to the beginning of the century might well have recalled the atmosphere which had brought into being the Triple Alliance and Triple Entente which had divided Europe into mutually hostile camps. It was as though deep underground disturbances were creating simultaneous tremors in all parts of the globe.

Despite the all-pervading atmosphere of gloomy apprehension, however, Chamberlain persisted in his policy of trying to accommodate the unaccommodatable. He was not alone. Franklin Roosevelt, the US President, was constrained by the Neutrality Act from involving his country in foreign entanglements. When Japanese ships on the Yangtze River sank the US gunboat *Panay*, Roosevelt was ready to accept a formal apology and to take the matter no further.

In his dealings with Germany, Chamberlain made one fundamental mistake. He believed, or allowed himself to be persuaded, that Hitler had genuine grievances and that, if they could be addressed, he would be satisfied. The peace settlement of 1919, in penalising the aggressor nations, had left Germany in a non-viable position. It had lost territory, including the valuable Rühr industrial region, and been left with an indefensible western boundary because it was forbidden to station troops in the Rhineland. In March 1936, however, when Hitler made his first territorial move – marching soldiers into the Rhineland – both France and Britain failed to respond, and he was allowed to get away with it. Many believe that had he been checked at this point the history of the following years would have been dramatically different. Henceforth he had only contempt for those who had failed

 to stand up to him and he boldly planned the next moves in his campaign to establish another great German empire: the Third Reich.

While Chamberlain declared himself willing to discuss Germany's problems with Hitler, his political opponents used every tactic to point out their mistrust of the appeasement policy. The focus of the anti-Chamberlain lobby was Winston Churchill. This veteran politician had held a variety of government posts between 1908 and 1929 but he was now widely regarded as both a hangover from a previous age and also a loose cannon. He frequently spoke in the Commons and published papers exposing Germany's military build-up but his following was small and Chamberlain believed he could ignore him. The Prime Minister felt secure in the knowledge that he had behind him a vast majority of the British people who were determined not to be embroiled in a conflict similar to that of 1914-18.

We should not let hindsight blind us to the realities of the time as they appeared to contemporary leaders. We, almost inevitably, think of the late 1930s as years of the build-up to World War II but, in 1937, Chamberlain and Roosevelt both had other worries on their minds which must have seemed at least as serious as the deteriorating foreign situation. The USA experienced a second Wall Street crash. In Britain the unemployment graph began to turn upwards once more. With their citizens worried about their jobs and feeding their families, Western leaders had immediate concerns to occupy them. The verdict of posterity was not at the forefront of their minds.

The further we get from the twentieth century the more clearly we can see what a bloody mess (literally) we made of it. It was the time when we in Europe went global with those squabbles with which we had been obsessed for over two hundred years. There was scarcely a corner of the planet which did not feel the impact of two murderous wars. One historian wrote that future ages would 'look back on the three decades between August 1914 and May 1945 as the era when Europe took leave of its senses'. Yet, even after 1945, when political leaders were able to count the cost of World War II in 50 million lost lives, hundreds of rubbled cities and the bankruptcy of national economies, they were unable to devise constructive new policies. Where the conflict between democracy and fascism left off, the conflict between communism and capitalism would take over, blighting lives, not only in a divided Europe, but in those regions emerging from colonial occupation, whose peoples were forced to enlist in an ideological war not of their own making. As if that were not bad enough, we all lived for decades under the mushroom cloud and the threat of annihilation. To discern a single 'turning-point' year which, for the people of Britain was particularly devoid of hope and replete with the menace of future disaster, is problematical. However, it does seem to me that 1936-7 was such a year. What was so cruel about it was that people's hopes were dashed just when the country seemed to be recovering from the national and international problems that had dogged it since the end of the 'war to end all wars'. Economic collapse loomed and, beyond it, the un-thinkable – a return to armed conflict.

HINDENBURG

In May 1937, for the first time in history, the cinema-going public were able to watch a horrifying international disaster taking place before their very eyes. The German airships, *Hindenburg* and *Graf Zeppelin*, had established regular trans-Atlantic passenger crossings. On 6 May 1937 the *Hindenburg* approached its mooring mast at Lakehurst, New Jersey at the end of a flight from Friedrichshafen. Seconds before docking a spark ignited the hydrogen-filled balloon. Immediately the craft became a giant fireball. As it crashed to the ground, passengers and crew scrambled from the gondola. Thirty-six people did not make it. The arrival was being filmed for a newsreel company. As soon as the celluloid reels arrived in Britain people flocked to see the report of the tragedy.

The loss of the *Hindenburg* delivered the *coup de grâce* to the era of commercial airship travel – a devastating demonstration that not all technological advance led the way to a better future. The airship age had begun in about 1900. Considerable excitement surrounded these craft which were the first heavier than air machines capable of controlled powered flight. During the First World War German airships (or dirigibles) used for bombing or reconnaissance raids had caused a panic in Britain out of all proportion to their effectiveness. And in the following years Britain and the USA had both developed airship programmes. The dirigible seemed to offer Britain a means of rapid transport between

London and distant outposts of empire. But problems always dogged the development of these unwieldy craft whose buoyancy depended on light, inflammable gas. After the Air Minister, Lord Thompson, was killed in another dirigible disaster, Britain wound down its programme.

As disasters go, the end of the Hindenburg was not a 'big story' but it certainly made a big impact because it became real and immediate for everyone who could afford the price of a cinema ticket and because it powerfully drove home the message of human fallibility.

What Happened Before...

1981-2   ROTTENEST YEAR

... And What Came After

1981-2

dictator *n* – a person exercising absolute authority of any kind…one who authoritatively prescribes a course of action or dictates what is to be done.

THAT'S THE DICTIONARY definition. Of course, we have to reach a long way back into our own past to discover a time when Britain was in thrall to such an autocrat, don't we? Limited monarchy and parliamentary democracy have tended to preserve us from having our freedoms trampled by any individual intent on achieving and exercising unrestricted power, *haven't they*? Let's have a close look at a period not so very long ago and see what answers it suggests to those questions.

Britain in the spring of 1981 was in a mess. The world was in the grip of economic recession. It was bad for everyone but Britain's record was worse than that of any of the other industrialised nations. Manufacturing industry was in decline. Interest rates were in the mid-teens. Unemployment was nudging three million. Labour relations were at an all time low. Racial tension in the inner cities was approaching breaking point. Paramilitary gangs ruled areas of Northern Ireland. Anarchy threatened. Precisely the kind of situation which, historically speaking, has tended to throw up extreme political solutions. Napoleon emerged from the chaos of the French Revolution. Hitler came to power because a demoralised Germany was looking for a saviour. Was Britain unconsciously seeking such a leader?

The trouble began in the spring of 1981 when racial tension in several inner cities exploded in violence. It was not as though concerned observers had not seen it coming. 'We have warned repeatedly about the unprecedented level of racist violence on the streets,' wrote the London Institute of Race Relations, 'and the continuous pressures put on black people – not the least of which is having constantly to prove, in any encounter with officialdom, their right even to be in Britain.'

By the 1980s a second generation of immigrants was being reared in what were effectively 'ghettoes'. Immigration from former colonies had continued at a steady rate and, inevitably, newcomers settled in localities where they already had friends and family. They grew up as Britons, knowing no other homeland, but feeling themselves marginalised as second-class citizens, discriminated against when they looked for jobs, education and housing. Worse still, when they were victimised by racist gangs, they were unable to rely on the police and local authorities for protection. Black youths reacted by forming their own gangs. Which in turn gave their white neighbours justification for their own grievances. White communities claimed that immigrants lowered the tone of their neighbourhoods. They felt intimidated by the black gangs whom they blamed for the increase of crime on their streets.

And somewhere in the middle of all this were police con-
stabularies, in many cases undermanned and ill-equipped to
deal with complex, potentially volatile situations.

On 6 April, the police in the south London area of Brixton launched a major 'clean-up' operation, code-named
'Swamp 81'. It involved more than a thousand people being
stopped, searched and questioned. The majority were from
ethnic minorities. Anger in the black community boiled over.
It only needed a single incident to shake the unstable social mix. On 10 April police assisting a black youth who had
been stabbed were set upon by an angry mob who believed
the young man was the victim of police brutality. That eve-
ning gangs were out on the streets looking for trouble.

The police chief sent out more officers. Confrontation
was now inevitable. Police cars were pelted with broken
paving slabs. Within hours, 46 officers had been injured. As
law and order broke down, shops were looted and business
premises torched. Fire engines and ambulances trying to
deal with the crisis came under attack. Twenty-four hours
after the original incident, television viewers were witness-
ing scenes on the streets of London that they had, hitherto,
only watched in reports from foreign capitals. Phalanxes of
policemen with riot shields and batons were in open warfare with mobs hurling bricks and petrol bombs. Not until 13
April did peace return to Brixton. It had taken 2,500 police
officers to achieve it.

The government appointed Lord Scarman, a senior
judge, to head up an inquiry into the disturbances. If they
thought that that would calm the situation they were soon
disillusioned.

Political responses were sharply divided. The Prime

Minister, Margaret Thatcher, pre-empted the Scarman Report by insisting that issues of race and unemployment had nothing to do with the problem; maverick Tory right-winger, Enoch Powell, disagreed, and campaigned for large-scale repatriation of immigrants. He was much closer to the truth when he warned, 'We've seen nothing yet.' The middle months of 1981 were a catalogue of disasters:

20 April: 15 police injured in fresh clashes with black groups in Finsbury Park, Ealing and Forest Gate, London.

13-14 June: Clashes between skinheads and black youths in Coventry led to over 80 arrests.

2 July: An Asian family in Walthamstow, London, murdered in an arson attack.

3-4 July: Racist skinheads assaulted an Indian woman in Southall, London. In retaliation an Asian mob burned down a local pub frequented by extremist white youths.

3-8 July: Fierce riots in Toxteth, Liverpool (See below.).

7 July: Police confronted large rival mobs in Wood Green, London.

8-10 July: Moss Side police station in Manchester attacked by a thousand rioters. Two days of street fighting followed.

9 July: Riots in Woolwich, London.

10 July: Serious disturbances in no less than 29 urban centres throughout Britain from Portsmouth to Edinburgh.
11-12 July: Riots in Bradford.
25 July: Police clashed with a thousand bikers in Keswick.

The worst scenes throughout these terrible weeks were those which occurred in Toxteth. The issue had, for a long time, been one of 'who controls the streets?' Estates with large concentrations of ethnic populations were virtually no-go areas to the forces of law and order. The police did not trust the black community and the feeling was mutual. Institutionalised racism certainly existed and the police were known to bend the rules in their zeal to 'clean up' the streets.

Once violence erupted there was no stopping it. Arson attacks on shops and business premises kept the emergency services constantly on the go. There was widespread looting. Brutality was met with brutality. CS gas was issued and used to disperse crowds. Some reports claimed that canisters were fired directly at rioters instead of over their heads. One man was knocked down and killed by a police vehicle. Over 460 policemen were injured. A hundred buildings were reduced to rubble. At the height of the trouble a visit by the Prime Minister was cancelled on security grounds. All public meetings and demonstrations throughout the country were banned – traditionally the first step on the road to the taking of emergency powers and the establishment of martial law.

Beyond doing that and calling for reports, the government was at a loss – and would remain so until they began properly to address the underlying causes of the malaise. Their attitude was challenged by no less a person than Lord Scarman. His report, published in November, implied some criticism of police methods and stated unequivocally, 'racial disadvantage is a fact of current British life'. This was not what the Tory government wished to hear – they were not the first or the last to ignore the recommendations of a report they had, themselves, commissioned.

In any case, they had many other things to worry about – the country was in a state of near economic collapse. The problems were complex and their solution called for well-thought-out responses to be applied to international and domestic policy. Unfortunately, it proved impossible to disentangle government action from doctrinaire economics and political prejudice. The British two-party system had driven itself into a cul-de-sac. It was still essentially a confrontation between the Labour Party, thought to represent the working class, and the Conservative Party, regarded as standing for the bosses.

Phalanxes of policemen with riot shields and batons were in open warfare with mobs hurling bricks and petrol bombs.

The Conservatives had come to power in 1979 and their economic policy was driven by two convictions; that government should not stifle individual enterprise by over-regulating industry and commerce and that the trade union movements wielded too much power. The results of their hands-off policy were catastrophic. With inflation running at eighteen per cent, wage claims were, inevitably, correspondingly high. This led to frequent acrimonious industrial disputes. The government urged employers to keep wage increases down while doing nothing to reflate the economy so that company profits would grow. By 1981 manufacturing output had declined by 30 per cent since 1978, unemployment had doubled to over three million and there was a mounting toll of bankruptcies (company liquidations would hit a record 12,000 in 1982). The non-interventionist policy, instead of bringing about a cut in government expenditure (another Tory objective), actually resulted in higher public spending. Take, for example, the nation's biggest single asset – North Sea oil. Exploitation of this natural resource brought the treasury about £8 billion a year in tax revenue and should have gone a long way towards enabling government to pay its way. In fact, more than half this precious income had to be paid out in increased unemployment and social benefits.

The problems facing the Prime Minister, Margaret Thatcher, were huge and complex. There were no easy answers. Many solutions were offered and she chose Alan Walters, a leading academic, as economics adviser. He was listened to and his advice followed even when the cabinet was united in opposition. On one occasion Thatcher supported Walters in the face of a letter to the press signed by 364 economists who pointed out his errors. The situation was reminiscent of that in royal courts of the seventeenth and eighteenth centuries when monarchs raised up their favourites and ignored the protests of their councils. In fact, that is a very apt comparison, for Mrs Thatcher's style of government was intensely personal. Her stubborn self-belief was a twentieth-century equivalent of the divine right of kings, the same messianic zeal that inspired the tyranny of Charles I and ultimately brought about his downfall. Her attitude towards opponents, often within her own cabinet and party, added a new word to the vocabulary – 'handbagging'.

The bedrock of Walters' policy was 'monetarism'. That, put simply, meant that the Treasury tackled inflation by controlling the supply of cash in circulation and bank deposits. Less money in people's pockets would theoretically slow down expenditure and prevent inflation, while managing any increase of the money supply would prevent the opposite evil of deflation. As far as the Prime Minister was concerned, double-figure inflation was *the* problem which had to be solved at all costs. Monetarism, she was convinced, was the sword that would sever the Gordian knot of the wage-price spiral (rising wage demands that increased manufacturing costs and thus boosted prices). The simplistic application of this doctrinaire economic theory had a disastrous impact. One aspect of it was that there was a natural level of unemployment and that it was not government's job to bring it down. Thus, any recovery would be built on the shattered lives of the poorer and more vulnerable members of society.

Another festering problem the government had to deal with was Northern Ireland. Sectarian discord had been rumbling for the best part of twenty years with increasingly frequent eruptions of violence. A new generation of Catholic citizens had grown up who were not prepared to continue suffering the humiliation of being treated as underdogs by the Protestant majority. The nationalist cause had been taken up by the Provisional IRA in 1969 and, in 1972, the regional government at Stormont had resigned, since when Ulster had been governed directly from Westminster. Various political initiatives came and went but there could be no agreement between Sinn Fein, the political wing of the IRA, who were set on union with the Irish Republic, and the Unionist parties, who were determined to preserve majority (i.e. Protestant) rule. Despite the growing number of British troops sent to restore order, several areas of the province had become virtually controlled by paramilitary gangs. Violent clashes and atrocities on all sides increased and the situation offered no glimmer of hope. The Tory government's attitude was that there could be no negotiation with 'terrorists'. They refused to regard Provisional activists as anything other than criminals. Matters came to a head early in 1981 with the case of a group of nationalists detained in the Maze prison. Led by Bobby Sands, they demanded to be treated as prisoners of war and when their demands were denied they went on hunger strike. Soon afterwards, the parliamentary seat at Fermanagh became vacant, and Sands, from his cell, contested it – and won. It was a tactical victory but the government remained firm. On 5 May, Sands died. He was the first of ten prisoners to starve themselves to death during the year. The nationalists now had martyrs and this boosted their support, even among more moderate Catholics – demonstrated when a fresh election was held in Fermanagh. Again the Sinn Fein candidate won. This marked a turning point in the nationalists' strategy. As well as causing mayhem on the streets, they would use legitimate political ends to demonstrate the level of support they possessed. There was no question of successful candidates taking up their Westminster seats. Sinn Fein did not recognise the legitimacy of the British government in Northern Ireland and its members certainly would not swear an oath of allegiance to the Queen. For their part, the government refused to recognise Sinn Fein's political legitimacy. They denied the party any right to present their case publicly. Radio and TV presenters were forbidden to interview them and press statements were strictly censored. Such an impasse was as oxygen to the men of violence. Their campaign now expanded to include London. A bomb planted outside the Chelsea army barracks killed two civilians and wounded forty others. Another device exploded in Oxford Street as a bomb disposal officer was trying to disarm it.

How on earth could a government sustain itself and get its legislation through parliament when its intractable and intransigent policies were so manifestly failing and when violence and anarchy were rampant? The answer is that normal parliamentary procedures were in disarray. The more the problems facing the country escalated, the more MPs disagreed about the way they should be tackled. When the Prime Minister took decisions without consulting colleagues and sacked some who questioned her, dissent rapidly spread to the back benches. In July 1981 an angry Prime Minister and Chancellor of the Exchequer faced a Cabinet revolt and were forced to abandon proposed expenditure cuts. Mrs Thatcher prided herself on her rock-like determination. She had boasted to the previous year's party conference, 'The lady's not for turning.' She was openly contemptuous of any who questioned her wisdom, referring to Tory dissidents as 'Wets', and ruthless about dismissing from office any who failed to toe the line. A cabinet purge in the summer was followed by a disastrous party conference in September, during which several ministers challenged Thatcher's policy proposals from the platform. In the autumn she was obliged to abandon some of her economic measures and she also came to the realisation that monetarism was not the answer to all ills. The lady, it seemed, *was* for turning – as long as she could do so quietly, without too many people noticing. Thatcher did, of course, have her supporters among the right wing of the party at large. Many of them were captivated by Thatcher's personality, and believed that strong leadership was, almost by definition, good leadership. When a nation is floundering and seems to have lost its way, the appearance of someone decisive at the helm is reassuring. However, her opponents in the party – who called themselves 'One-nation Tories' – believed that their leader's policies were draconian and divisive. The Conservative Party was split.

And what was the Labour Party doing all this time? The answer is 'disintegrating'. Like the Conservatives, Labour members were divided between those committed to traditional ideology and procedures and those who wished the party to respond to the challenges of a changing world. But, where the Conservatives had a strong and autocratic leader, Labour at the time was in the hands of a weak, muddled chief, in the form of Michael Foot, who continually bowed before the democratic demands of internal factions.

Labour's roots were in the industrial heartlands and the trade union movement – a constituency which, in May 1981, made a deliberate and nostalgic appeal to the past. Thousands of men and women took part in the 'People's March for Jobs'. It replicated the Jarrow Crusade of 1936 but its mood was very different from the earlier, almost genteel, event. The protestors spent four weeks travelling from Liverpool to London bearing banners with such slogans as JOBS NOT BOMBS (a reference to government expenditure on nuclear weapons), SACK THE TORIES, THREE MILLION UNEMPLOYED SCANDAL. The march culminated in Trafalgar Square with a rally attended by 100,000 protestors. By this time left wingers and traditionalists in the Labour Party had made a significant gain, having obtained a change to the party's constitution which took the election of the leader out of the hands of Labour MPs and gave more power to the unions and constituency members.

This was all too much for the right wing of the Labour Party. In March a small group of MPs broke away and formed the Social Democratic Party, the first new political force to emerge in Britain for almost 90 years (the Independent Labour Party had been founded in 1893). 'Force' is not too strong a word. The SDP tapped into a prevailing mood of widespread disillusion with the major parties. By the end of the year 25 defectors (including one from the Conservatives) had joined the SDP, opinion polls credited it with 50 per cent support among the electorate and it had won its first by-election. Furthermore, talks with the Liberal Party had resulted in the creation of the SDP-Liberal Alliance. Three-party politics had arrived in Britain and pundits began arguing about the 'threat' of hung parliaments and weak coalitions.

Electoral considerations aside, what the rush of support for the new party demonstrated was a sense of 'lostness' and confusion in the country. Britain was finding it hard to detect a new role in a changing world. It had, by now, said a reluctant 'Goodbye' to empire and a distinctly muted 'Hello' to the European Economic Community (forerunner of the European Union). Thatcher's predecessor, Edward Heath (for whom she entertained a powerful loathing), had taken the UK into the EEC in 1973, although the Conservatives were less than enthusiastic about British membership. To some it seemed that Britain had ended up with the worst of all worlds. An open-door policy to citizens of the Commonwealth had helped to fuel racial disharmony which now loomed as a major problem. At the same time the partial surrender of sovereignty to the European parliament had stirred up nationalist feeling. Many of Thatcher's colleagues left no-one in any doubt that they wanted out. Early in 1981 the Prime Minister had a very frosty series of meetings with her EEC counterparts on the subject of contributions to the Community's budget. The stark choice was between, on the one hand, enthusiastic efforts to make the European ideal work (even, as some Europhiles urged, to take a leadership role in the Community) and, on the other hand, economic isolation. Few people actually wanted to face that choice.

Even more fundamental to the nation's malaise, however, were the changes taking place in the world economy. Britain's strong position in international markets had traditionally been based on manufacturing exports. For over a hundred years this had sustained the iron and steel and coal industries which, together with the production of cars, railway stock, metal tools and machine parts, had provided employment for millions of citizens. But these industries were based on old technology and old market conditions. By the 1980s, powerful competitor nations – Germany, Japan, the USA, India, China – were encroaching upon Britain's share in what was, in any case, a declining market. The future lay with new technology – the transistor, the microchip, the home and office computer. 1981 was the year that saw the marketing of both an affordable personal computer and the first portable computer (roughly the weight of a modern desktop model). This revolutionary technology had been developed in the USA – in 1982 Microsoft would set up a British subsidiary. If Britain was to catch up it would be little use pouring money into the rescuing of traditional manufacturing. The main hope for many of the unemployed and those under the threat of redundancy would lie in retraining, to produce the hardware and software on which all business and industry, not to mention government and public services, would, in future, depend. But few members of the labour force were prepared to embrace such radical thinking and trade unions concentrated their efforts on trying to save their members' jobs. Even the Conservatives were disinclined to confront the massed ranks of the major unions. Instead, the government spent considerable sums shoring up the British Steel Corporation and British Leyland (a nationalised enterprise), and, when the Coal Board recommended the closing of 23 pits in order to streamline the industry and reduce the stockpiling of unsold coal, it put off its decision for fear of provoking a damaging and costly strike.

Another controversy undermining the government's popularity was the deployment of nuclear weapons on British soil. Most people believed that Britain should have its own nuclear deterrent carried on Polaris submarines and did not support the Labour Party's call for unilateral renunciation. But the location of a new generation of American Trident missiles in England was another matter. The Campaign for Nuclear Disarmament, a movement which had been very vociferous in the early 1960s but had been almost moribund for the best part of a decade, now sprang to life with a mass rally in London in October.

All in all, then, by the end of 1981 the prevailing mood was grim and getting grimmer. Only one event had filtered some sunlight through the gloom. In July the heir to the throne, Prince Charles, was married to Lady Diana Spencer, the 'people's princess'. It was a fairy-tale wedding climaxing a courtship that had been avidly followed by the national and international press. The great day witnessed the kind of spectacle that Britain does better than anyone else. Record crowds turned out to cheer the carriages through the streets to St Paul's Cathedral. Millions more watched the ceremony on television.

1982 opened with little prospect of improvement on any front. Unemployment continued rising and reached a peak of three and a quarter million. Industrial output went on falling and Britain's share of international trade declined by 35 per cent between 1978 and 1982. By the spring the three political parties were running neck and neck in the opinion polls. With two years at most before a general election, Margaret Thatcher might well have been hoping that Labour's problems would continue and that the people's love affair with the Alliance might cool. Failing that, only a miracle could save the Tories from certain defeat. Salvation came in the person of a tin-pot South American dictator.

Deep in the chilly South Atlantic, some 500 kilometres off the coast of Argentina, lay a group of islands known as the Falklands. Its population was less than 2,000 and its slender economy depended entirely on sheep farming. In 1981, if you had asked anyone in Britain what he or she knew about these remote islands, the chances are that the response would have been a blank stare. The result would very likely have been the same if you had quizzed members of parliament. The British as a nation knew little and cared less about the Falkland Islands. A year later everyone knew about them – and some even cared. Insignificant as these treeless, rainswept settlements were, they were part of the last vestiges of the British Empire and that invested them with a certain emotional significance. Back in the days of colonial competition, the islands had been claimed by both Britain and Spain, but since 1833 British sovereignty had not been seriously challenged. However, successive rulers of Argentina, independent since 1816, considered that they had inherited ownership of the Falklands (which they called the Malvinas) from Spain. It was certainly true that the islanders were more dependent on the nearby mainland than on the 'mother' country, some 13,000 kilometres distant. Sporadic diplomatic discussions took place over the years and, in 1980, a fresh round of talks had been held to consider some kind of mutually acceptable accommodation.

Two factors turned diplomatic activity into military conflict. In Argentina economic near-collapse had led, in 1980, to noisy demonstrations against the unpopular dictator, Leopoldo Galtieri. He desperately needed a diversion to take the people's minds off his domestic policies and decided that a display of strength in foreign policy would unite his people behind him.

At the same time Thatcher's cabinet was reviewing its defence strategy. The loss of overseas territories had considerably diminished the navy's role and the cash-strapped government decided to downsize it. Designated ships would be sold off or retired. One of the proposed economies was to call home HMS *Endurance*, the only vessel on patrol duty in the South Atlantic. In late February, a new round of talks about sovereignty began in New York. All this encouraged Galtieri to think that he could get away with a grab for the Falklands. He believed that Britain had neither the resources nor the will to put up a fight. A month later, British intelligence passed on to the government a report that Argentina was preparing an invasion but Thatcher chose to ignore it. What she did do was ask the US President, Ronald Reagan, to bring pressure to bear on the Galtieri regime. However, in Buenos Aires plans were too far advanced to be halted. On 2 April the Argentine invasion of the Falklands began.

Britain had not sought the quarrel but, once the gauntlet had been thrown down, it had no alternative but to take it up. When Thatcher ordered a task force to sail to the Falklands to combat Argentinian aggression, she had the backing of all parties. The response would have been the same whoever had been the current prime minister, though it is possible that a less truculent leader might more readily have found a diplomatic solution. However, it was the 'Iron Lady' whose reputation received a boost from the crisis. She draped herself in the Union flag and was portrayed in the pro-Tory press as Britannia, the embodiment of the national spirit, a reincarnated Boudicca. She took every political advantage from the situation, castigating the 'evil' Argentinian junta in speeches and grabbing opportunities to be photographed with 'her' troops. Public opinion, led by the press, was divided. The *Sun* newspaper mounted a xenophobic attack on the 'Argies', to which the anti-war *Mirror* responded with equally virulent denunciation of the 'warmongering' Prime Minister. The responsible organs of the press took a more sombre stance in reporting a conflict which, whatever the rights and wrongs of the issues, was being paid for with the blood of young servicemen and servicewomen on both sides.

The Falklands War was an unequal contest. Argentina had the advantage of proximity to the battle zone but it was a third-rate military power and, once the British task force had reached the islands, superior training, discipline and equipment proved their worth. The war lasted 74 days and cost the lives of 258 British (more than in the later Iraq War) and 649 Argentinian service personnel. Apart from the incalculable toll of physical and psychological injury, Britain had to foot a bill of almost £3 billion for rescuing its tiny colony. Another Agincourt or Trafalgar the Falklands campaign was not, but, like those famous battles, it had the advantage of being a very simple one to understand. A peaceful people had suffered unprovoked attack and that attack had been repulsed. Whatever the merits of the competing Argentinian and British claims, in military terms it was easy to identify the good guys and the bad guys. Perhaps surprisingly, victory in the South Atlantic did not quite produce the wave of nationalistic euphoria the government might have hoped for. This came home to the Prime Minister at the thanksgiving service at St Paul's Cathedral when, instead of taking a triumphalist stance, the Archbishop of Canterbury sombrely remembered the dead and wounded of *both* sides. Mrs Thatcher was decidedly unamused.

What it did do was mark a significant upturn in the Prime Minister's fortunes. This last defiant waving of the imperialist flag served as a morale booster for many British people, especially older citizens who could remember their school days when world maps were dotted with red splodges marking the multitude of Britain's overseas possessions. They had subsequently seen virtually all these territories gain their independence. Their proud nation had shrunk in power and significance.

MARGARET THATCHER

Now, at last, the old lion had given one last roar. When the danger was well past, Mrs T paid a visit to the Falklands and she presided at a victory parade when the troops returned (a parade from which the wounded were excluded so as not to spoil the desired image). She now began to see herself as a great war leader, in the mould of Winston Churchill – a delusion encouraged by her increasing popularity. Boosted by the feel-good factor, the Conservatives moved ahead in the opinion polls and the Prime Minister felt ready to take on all comers. She steered new trades union legislation through the Commons, which made the unions liable, under certain circumstances, for prosecution in civil law for losses incurred by employers as a result of industrial action. And in head-to-head confrontations with nurses, railway staff and coal miners the government now stood firm. Intransigence would be the mark of the Thatcher years from then on. Having eaten Galtieri for breakfast, the Iron Lady was ready for her next meal.

On the other side, Labour continued to immolate itself with its internal squabbles. As a potential leader of the country, Michael Foot looked anaemic beside the effulgent lady who gloated at him from the opposite despatch box. As for the SDP-Liberal Alliance, the war had deprived it of the oxygen of publicity. The party continued to make gains in by-elections but the excitement of the previous year had passed. Instead of being perceived by many as a force for change, what the Alliance had become in electoral terms was a group which divided, and therefore weakened, the opposition to the Conservatives. The cabinet began to make serious plans for what would have seemed suicidal a few months earlier – a general election in 1983 – although beneath the shift of mood nothing else had really changed. Unemployment, poverty, inflation, industrial decline, the Northern Ireland troubles – these were still the realities with which many Britons were having to contend in the grim year 1982.

***

So *does* our constitution give us sufficient protection against the possibility of dictatorship emerging in a modern democracy? Did the events of 1981-2 highlight serious flaws in our system? Margaret Thatcher was *voted* into office. She *had* a popular mandate. But history teaches us that that, of itself, is no safeguard against the emergence of tyrants. Adolf Hitler was elected into office but made himself powerful enough to overthrow the constitution of the Weimar Republic with all its built-in checks and balances. He is not the only leader to have received power from the people and then used it as a weapon against them.

Sometimes a nation needs a leader with a clear vision and the strength of character to force the kind of change that more cautious politicians lack the will to bring about. It is time that vindicates or condemns their actions. The jury is still out on Margaret Thatcher's premiership and it is unlikely that any agreed verdict will ever be reached. But that is not my concern in this essay. I have merely tried to recreate something of what life in 1981-2 Britain felt like *at the time.* We all know that Mrs Thatcher did not become a tyrant in the long term. She overstepped the mark and received the *coup de grâce* from her own parliamentary party. She did not, as other dictators have done, overthrow the constitution and proclaim herself prime minister for life. But for a few years she was, if not exactly a dictator, certainly an autocrat. She did not operate by persuasion. She saw no need to woo opponents in order to bring them round to her point of view. She dictated 'What is to be done'.

But for a charismatic leader to get away with assuming autocratic powers two other things are necessary – a sense of national crisis and an ineffective opposition. Unfortunately both were apparent in this rotten year.

WE WON THE ASHES!

If Britain needed a fillip in the summer of 1981, it was provided for them by the champions of what was still regarded as the national game. The England-Australia Test match series of that year has gone down in cricketing legend.

Ian Botham, England's great all-rounder, captained the team, but after the first two matches resigned the post, the better to focus on his playing. The teams next met on 16 July at Headingley, Leeds, and in the first innings England mustered just 174 in response to Australia's 401. England were forced to follow on and, at 105 for 5, seemed to be heading for humiliation. Enter Botham, who proceeded to crash his way to 149 not out. Australia now only needed 130 to go two up in the series. In one of the most tense finishes the game has ever seen, the tourists were bowled out for 121. The series was level and all to play for.

At Edgbaston, Birmingham (30 July – 2 August, Australia seemed set for revenge. After the first innings they had a 69-run lead and then bowled England out in the second for 219. They had plenty of time to knock off the 151 runs necessary for victory, and at 104 for 5 were coasting. Enter Botham. In one of the most astonishing spells of bowling ever seen, he took all five remaining Australian wickets for only one run. England won by 29 runs.

A further English victory at Old Trafford, Manchester, in which Botham scored 118 off 102 deliveries, gave England a rare victory over the old enemy. Britain had found the phenomenon it needed to raise spirits and stir the blood – a hero.